MW01225289

To Our Readers:

INTRODUCING

OTABIND®

INTERNATIONAL

"The Book That Lies Flat"
— *User Friendly Binding* —

This title has been bound using state-of-the-art **OtaBind®** technology.

- The spine is 3-5 times stronger than conventional perfect binding
- The book lies open flat, regardless of the page being read
- The spine floats freely and remains crease-free even with repeated use

We are pleased to be able to bring this new technology to our customers.

 **Health Communications, Inc.**

3201 S.W. 15th Street
Deerfield Beach, FL 33442-8190
(305) 360-0909

OTABIND®

INTERNATIONAL

The Netherlands

DATE RAPE
The Secret Epidemic

- What It Is
- What It Isn't
- What It Does To You
- What You Can Do About It

Marcia Mobilia Boumil, J.D., LL.M.
Joel Friedman, Ph.D.
Barbara Ewert Taylor, J.D.

Health Communications, Inc.
Deerfield Beach, Florida

Library of Congress Cataloging-in-Publication Data

Boumil, Marcia
    Date rape: what it is, what it isn't, what it does to you, what
you can do about it / Joel Friedman, Marcia M. Boumil, Barbara
Ewert Taylor.
        p. cm.
    Includes bibliographical references.
    ISBN 1-55874-252-2
    1. Acquaintance rape — United States. I. Boumil, Marcia
Mobilia. II. Taylor, Barbara Ewert. III. Title.
HV6561.F73 1992
362.88'3—dc20   92-24163
                                                                      CIP

© 1993 Marcia M. Boumil, Joel Friedman, Barbara E. Taylor
ISBN 1-55874-252-2

Publisher: Health Communications, Inc.
               3201 S.W. 15th Street
               Deerfield Beach, Florida 33442-8190

Cover design by Iris T. Slones

DEDICATION

To Patricia Bowman and Desiree Washington, and to other courageous women, because they came forward.

The Women And Law Series

CONTENTS

PREFACE

Approximately every five minutes a woman in the United States reports to the police that she has been raped. Many experts think the actual number of rapes is as much as 20 times higher. Statistics concerning the incidence of rape within the industrialized countries that keep records indicate that women living in large United States cities are more likely to be at risk for rape than anywhere else in the world. Statistical surveys from San Francisco and Chicago suggest that the incidence of rape ranges from one in five to one in three who will be victims of incest, marital rape, violent rape or date rape sometime during their lives.

While many people believe that most rapes occur from the attack of a stranger, the facts indicate that most rapes are perpetrated by an acquaintance of the victim. While those perpetrated by strangers are the ones most often reported, studies done on college campuses suggest that less than one in 100 rapes that occur between acquaintances are ever reported to the police. The numbers are staggering. The costs to society are extraordinary. The disastrous consequences for many, and perhaps most, victims last for a lifetime. Hundreds of thousands, if not millions, of women in the United States today, right now, are victims. Millions more will become victims.

The authors anticipate that most people reading this book are not doing so merely by chance. With the startling number of victims, it is more than likely that you are reading this because of a personal interest in the problem. Either you yourself or someone close to you would probably benefit from having as much information as possible. "Knowledge is power" and this book is designed to empower you with the information you need to know about the specific form of rape known as acquaintance rape, campus rape, confidence rape and, more popularly, date rape.

What we are referring to is forced sexual activity, intercourse or other sexual acts, that occur between a victim and a perpetrator who know each other. The forced sexual activity occurs mainly in the home, apartment, dormitory, hotel room or car of one of the parties. The incident may last for a period of hours and often involves the use of alcohol or drugs. Unlike victims of violent rape, date rape victims often delay in seeking help and are more reluctant to report the crime. They often feel shame and guilt and may be confused as to whether or not rape actually occurred and, if it did, whether they induced or brought it on themselves.

From May, 1991, to February, 1992, the public was stunned by two dramatic and highly visible rape trials. The first was that of William Kennedy Smith, a young doctor, nephew of Senator Ted Kennedy, a member of upper class U.S.A. The other was the rape trial of Mike Tyson, the ghetto bad boy who rose to become the heavyweight boxing champion of the world. Both cases are examples of date rape and, as never before, presented the world with detailed real life examples of all the elements involved in date rape and date rape legal procedures. The public, through live televised trials and extensive media coverage, has been able to see what date rape is. The real life drama portrayed how this traumatic event affects the victim and how confusing it can be to those of us who attempt to understand what, how and why these events occurred.

To understand this type of trauma we need to step out of purely logical thinking and instead try to relate to the actual experience of being forced to perform sexual acts. How do we explain a victim's lapses in memory or why she might remain for a time at the place she claims she was raped instead of running away? Why is information about a victim's past, particularly her sexual history, excluded from the trial? What legal procedures allow the accused to get away without making a pretrial statement or deposition while the victim and her witnesses must report what happened in vivid detail, only to later have that testimony used to damage their credibility when they may not remember those details months later at trial.

This book will answer these and other important questions. It will explain what date rape is, why it happens, what can be done about it and what victims need to know when confronted with the legal process. It will highlight the trends of the law concerning the prosecution of date rape.

Because a few courageous women have come forward to confront their abusers, the whole area of forced sexual activity has been opened up for public examination and understanding. What was once kept hidden as a shameful secret is now out in the open and helping to shed new light on this enormous problem. Old myths are being destroyed and women now are able to arm themselves with information and shared experience. The abusers may be bigger and stronger but victims need no longer feel that they are without recourse. Remember — "knowledge is power". We hope this book will empower you.

Marcia Mobilia Boumil
Senior Author

CHAPTER ONE

What Date Rape Is: When No Means No

Katie was raped repeatedly over a period of several hours by a man whom she had dated years earlier. Although angry about the attack, she didn't want to press charges except that she was terrified that the rapist might have AIDS. Since she had known him, Katie was aware of his lifestyle, including his use of intravenous drugs, and was worried that he might be HIV positive and could have transmitted the infection to her. However, Katie was ultimately advised that her state was not among the few states requiring mandatory AIDS testing of sex crime defendants. If she chose to be tested, both the expense of testing and the consequences were hers to bear alone.

The criminal justice system recognizes rape as one of the most violent, dangerous and degrading physical acts that one human being can commit against another. It can be sudden and unpredictable, or it can extend over a long period of time. It can be committed by a total stranger or by a close family member, friend, acquaintance or date in the context of a trusted relationship. It does not discriminate. The victims come from all walks of life. They can be young or old, married or single, rich or poor. A victim could be you or I. What all rape victims have in common is that they are victims of anger, power and aggression at the hands of a man who uses his sexuality as a weapon to terrorize and brutalize. A victim who resists may pay with her life. Even those who survive are likely to be affected by the experience for the rest of their lives.

What Is Rape?

The frequency with which rape occurs is startling. Experts seem to agree that a vast majority of rapes go unreported, but among those reported, one study indicates that there are 16 attempted rapes and 10 completed rapes in the United States every hour (*U.S. House Report*, 1990). The same study indicates that the actual rate of rape is probably tenfold, resulting in 100 completed rapes each hour. This also means that any woman faces an overall likelihood of between 15% and 40% that she will be the victim of an attempted or actual rape sometime during her life.

The definition of rape is relatively simple, but the implications, both behavioral and psychological, are enormously complicated. A woman is raped when she is compelled by implicit or explicit threat of force or violence to submit to or participate in a sexual act, including but not limited to sexual intercourse. It can occur in a number of contexts, not all of which immediately appear to be violent. Nevertheless, it is usually motivated by the perpetrator's desire to achieve dominance and control over his victim by intimidating or brutalizing her until she submits to his acts of sexual aggression. Rape may take various forms:

Stranger Or "Blitz" Rape

This is the type of rape people usually think of when referring to "rape." Most people envision a rapist as an unknown man who jumps out of the bushes in a secluded place late at night wielding a knife and threatening his victim with violence. The victim is caught off guard and may or may not resist the attack, depending upon how terrified she is and whether she perceives that it may help. (If there is no one around, there is little to be accomplished by screaming.) This is called stranger or "blitz" rape.

Rape by a stranger can occur in a victim's home or car; it can happen outside by a surprise assault; it can occur in any other place where a potential victim can be found or forced to go by the threat of her attacker. The rapist often uses a weapon to threaten and coerce the victim. A victim can be forced to perform or submit to any physical acts of a sexual nature usually, but not always, including sexual intercourse.

Date Or "Confidence" Rape

Date or acquaintance rape generally involves the same type of forced sexual behavior, but the perpetrator is known to the victim and there has usually been some sort of ongoing social relationship between them. It can be as brief as meeting at a bar and leaving with the acquaintance or as lengthy as a long-term dating or cohabiting relationship. It can also be committed by a person with whom the victim is acquainted but has had no prior social activity, such as a co-worker or a neighbor. The crucial distinction from stranger rape is that there must be some basis for an ongoing relationship that creates an element of trust ("confidence") in the victim.

Date rape typically occurs in the victim's or perpetrator's home or car. Both individuals are likely to have been using alcohol and/or drugs, and the incident may last over a period of hours, during which the victim has gradually become aware of the danger. The victim's subsequent experience of shame, guilt and reluctance to seek help often leads to the under-reporting of this crime. Campus rape is a related offense which is identified essentially the same way as confidence or date rape, except that it occurs in a campus environment usually between students who know each other, are dating or attending parties together.

Marital Rape

Throughout legal history most jurisdictions have excluded from the definition of rape the possibility that a man could rape his wife. There are a number of historical reasons for this but the most obvious was that a wife was considered the property of her husband and had no right to deny him sexual pleasure. The law was also thought to promote domestic harmony by refusing to prosecute a man who was said to have forced himself on his wife. Today most jurisdictions have amended their statutes to eliminate the exclusion for married partners, and a number of communities have prosecuted men for this crime. As in any rape, the important element is that the victim did not consent, and undoubtedly she carries the heavy burden of proving that she did not consent and that it was communicated to her husband who thereafter acted anyway, forcing sex on her in disregard of her stated objection. Convictions for this crime are still difficult to obtain unless the couple is separated or divorced and other violent acts accompany the rape.

Statutory Rape

Unlike other forms of rape, statutory rape usually refers to consensual sexual activity including intercourse between a male of any age and a girl who is under a certain age, which the jurisdiction designates by statute as necessary for her consent. This varies from one jurisdiction to another, but most set the statutory age of consent between 13 and 16. If the girl is under the statutory age necessary for consent, even if she willingly participated, the male who engages her in sexual activity is guilty of statutory rape. It is also no defense that he did not know that she was underage; the law considers it to be the man's responsibility to make substantial efforts to determine the age of his partner.

The term "statutory" in statutory rape means that the law will call the act rape regardless of whether or not the victim was willing because that victim is considered legally unable to give "meaningful consent," either by virtue of her age or physical condition. Every state has a law or laws which set a minimum age at which this consent can be given, how old the victim can be before the law will consider her to be old enough to know what she is doing. This minimum age of consent is not related to the so-called "age of majority" which is now 18, the minimum age at which a person can vote and be bound by other legal acts such as taking out a loan to pay for a car (but not the age at which a person can purchase and drink alcohol).

Statutory rape laws exist in every state. The purpose of these laws is both to protect underage children and to deter those who would take advantage of their youth. Although these laws may differ in details from state to state, they all share the significant similarity in saying that it doesn't matter how willing the victim was. If she was below that state's minimum age of consent, the crime is still rape. Additionally, if the victim was both below the minimum age and not willing, the crime is not only statutory rape, but can also be classified as "child molestation" or "child sexual abuse." The penalties for statutory rape can be as severe as or more severe than those for rape of an adult, and the penalties for the additional crime of "child sexual abuse" are virtually always more severe, especially when the victim is quite young.

Social Myths And Societal Stigmas

A variety of social myths about the types of women who are victimized by rape have evolved over the past several decades, many of which have encouraged women to deny that the attack ever occurred and never report it. Such myths revolve around the belief that victims of rape are sexually promiscuous and somehow asked for or deserved to be attacked. Other unfounded stereotypes include the notion that typical rape victims are of low socioeconomic status, poorly educated and emotionally unstable. Some common myths are the following:

- Rape victims are usually beautiful young women who invite rape through their careless behavior.
- Rape victims are promiscuous women who provoke attacks.
- Women can do nothing to fend off sexual assaults, so they might as well enjoy it.
- A woman who accompanies a man to his home is willing to have sex or should expect to have sex.
- Women who charge men with rape are out to get revenge on a man.
- Women provoke rape by wearing revealing clothing and acting "loose."
- A woman can avoid being raped if she wants to.

These myths, however untrue, have led police and prosecutors to be very selective about the cases they choose to pursue. A study analyzing the Canadian criminal justice system found that the police consistently classified complaints by professional women as "founded," while at the same time those by victims who were unemployed or on welfare were one-third more likely to have their complaints classified as "unfounded." In another study in New York City, 33% of the alleged rapes by a stranger resulted in an indictment while only 7% of acquaintance (date) rape cases had a similar result.

Some of the social myths regarding rape became the focus of a reform movement in the 1970s when a majority of states enacted legislation to protect victims from inflammatory and prejudicial attacks. This was done to encourage victims to come forward without fear that the cost of pursuing their attackers would be unwarranted inquiries about their sexual history or attacks on their chastity or credibility. The result was various forms of "rape shield laws" that minimize inquiry into a victim's personal history.

In the 1970s there was growing criticism of the legal system's obvious bias against many rape victims because of the myths that had by then become institutionalized in the way rape cases were handled by the police and prosecutors. In their substantial reform efforts, many states revised existing rape laws. Some common revisions included:

1. Classifying rape as a sex-neutral offense

2. Redefining rape as "sexual assault" or "sexual battery"

3. Re-evaluating whether and under what circumstances a victim should be expected to resist her attacker

4. Eliminating the exception for spouses, thereby allowing the cause of action for marital rape

5. Re-evaluating the need for a victim to produce supporting evidence (in addition to her own testimony) that the rape actually occurred

6. Re-defining the crime of "rape" to include other sexual acts in addition to vaginal penetration.

Since the adoption of many of these changes by various states, it has become easier for victims to come forward and testify against their rapists. Nevertheless, the particular form of rape known as date rape is still the most difficult to prosecute. In this case, the perpetrator's defense is almost always that the victim consented and the burden of proof is on the prosecution.

Reaching Out For Help

Rape victims can expect a variety of responses from the law enforcement, medical, legal and counseling personnel who attend to their cases. On the one hand, there are kind, caring and competent professionals who seek to assist victims and bring their assailants to justice; on the other hand, there are prejudiced, inexperienced, overworked and insensitive individuals who allow the system to continue to betray a victim by failing to acknowledge and attend to her needs.

- Shortly after Jill was raped at knife point, she took a taxi to her local police department. It was approximately 1:30 a.m. and the only officer on duty was a rookie who had no prior experience with sex crime victims. He interviewed Jill for about 40 minutes, listening to her story and occasionally interrupting her with questions. At times he appeared impatient as Jill couldn't recall what the attacker looked like or what he said to her. Her demeanor was at times hysterical and incoherent. When she finished her story, Jill asked how the police would handle her complaint. The officer commented that rape cases are difficult to prosecute, particularly when the victim cannot even recall the basic facts such as the assailant's identity. By the time a rape investigator contacted her the next morning, Jill was already discouraged about prosecuting the attacker. She was never examined by any medical personnel as the officer had sent her home, apparently assessing her case as too difficult to pursue.

- When Debbie was raped by a man whom she had met at a nightclub, she contacted a rape crisis hotline and was directed to her local emergency room to document her injuries. She arrived at approximately 10:05 p.m. and was kept waiting for almost two hours before being seen. She had not yet decided whether to go to the police, but the choice was taken away from her when the hospital informed her that if she wanted to be treated, the assault had to be reported. By the time she was actually examined, Debbie had become calm and focused and was able to describe in great detail how the attack occurred and what physical trauma she had sustained. She had no obvious bruises or cuts, although semen was found. In talking to the medical intern about her reluctance to go to the police, Debbie received the impression that he believed she had consented to sex, must have changed her mind afterward and would never be able to convince anyone that she was sexually assaulted.

- Linda was raped by a man she had dated once but declined to see again. Her complaint made it to the district attorney's office as she apparently seemed to be a good witness with a credible story. There were no inconsistencies with the police report filed weeks earlier. Nevertheless, she was warned that "acquaintance rape" is difficult to prosecute and a case that isn't foolproof will be rejected.

During the trial the defense attorney commented on her "attractive appearance" and inquired extensively about her dating history, making untrue references to her sexual history and alleged illegal drug use. He even tried to insinuate that she had been molested years earlier by an uncle. He badgered her

repeatedly to try to prove that she had consented to
sex with the defendant. By the time her testimony
ended, Linda felt raped again and regretted that she
had pressed charges.

• After Lisa underwent the physical exam conducted by
the rape trauma team, she was greeted by Ellen, a
rape crisis volunteer whose function was to help victims deal with the psychological trauma of sexual assault. Ellen was herself a rape victim and believed
that she could help Lisa by listening to her story as
well as sharing her own of several years earlier. Since
Lisa could not afford private counseling, she was grate-
ful to Ellen. Nevertheless, she ultimately found the
experience was not particularly helpful since Ellen
seemed to be "stuck" in her own traumatic experience
and was unable to assist Lisa with working through
her own very different experience.

The above are examples of issues confronting rape victims. After the attack, a victim has a number of options
available in terms of finding help and attempting to prosecute her assailant. Depending on her situation (and her
luck), the avenues of approach may yield unpredictable
results. The victim (now "survivor") confronts the criminal justice system (police, district attorney who "prose-
cutes" her case and the courts) and the medical community
(physicians who perform medical exams and rape crisis
counselors). Each presents challenges to the victim. The
order in which they are presented, particularly the first
two, may be reversed. That is, a woman may choose first
to go to the police and thereafter go for medical attention;
she may also seek medical attention first and follow up
with the police.

The First Stop: The Police

One of the most basic problems with the way the system treats rape victims begins with their reporting of the

crime to the police. A victim traumatized by one of the
most vicious and insidious crimes imaginable ought to be
able to expect law enforcement personnel to be knowl-
edgeable, compassionate and eager to see justice done.
Too often the victim begins the process with a male police
officer, often inexperienced in general police work, who
may never have investigated a sexual assault, but whose
judgment about her will be given great weight in the
ultimate determination of whether her case should go
forward and be prosecuted. His assessment of the legitimacy of the complaint, based upon his impression of the
victim's credibility, is extremely difficult to change, even if
he has little or no experience with rape and probably has
his own prejudices about rape victims. The police are
particularly leery of date rape cases, and, if the victim
admits to the presence or use of drugs or alcohol, her case
is immediately suspect. To the police, drug or alcohol use
indicates impaired character and low morals, leading to
the conclusion that she originally consented, was asking
for it or somehow behaved in a manner that, if not deserved, then excused the sexual assault.

In making the initial determination on the victim's credibility (which later will become difficult to change), an
inexperienced police officer may give great weight to a
woman's dress, attractiveness and, most importantly, the
clarity and consistency of her report in judging her credibility. In spite of the diminished coherence that is often
present in the aftermath of such a trauma, the victim's
memory lapses or contradictions may severely affect the
police officer's assessment of legitimacy.

Date rape in particular seems prone to the highest degree of police suspicion. Many officers seem to believe
that women are raped by their dates, but have asked for
it or participated in the act. Either the woman encouraged
the attack by dating a man and leading him on, or she
must be a "loose" woman who uses poor discretion in
selecting dates. Or, if it was a long-term relationship, she

must have resisted ending a destructive relationship and thereby precipitated the assault. Some officers even believe certain women are prone to being victimized (i.e., those with low socioeconomic status or limited intelligence) and their cases are less worthy of prosecution. The police are also often responsible for whether a victim receives a medical exam, which ultimately provides invaluable evidence if the crime is prosecuted. If the intake officer believes that a particular case is meritorious, he will send or escort the victim to a local hospital or rape crisis center. The physical evidence of an immediate examination, including the presence (or absence) of rape trauma syndrome (discussed in Chapter 5) cannot easily be obtained even a few hours later. If, on the other hand, the police initially believe the case to be unfounded, a medical exam may never be suggested. This leaves the victim with unconfirmed symptoms and great difficulty in ultimately having her case prosecuted.

The first stop at the police station not only affects whether a perpetrator is apprehended and brought to justice, preventing future crimes, but may also affect the ultimate adjustment that the victim makes to cope with the trauma. A lack of sensitivity or decisionmaking based upon prejudice, inexperience, ignorance or lack of case management can thwart justice, leave a violent criminal on the streets and severely affect the victim's recovery.

The Second Stop: Medical Attention

Women who seek medical attention first may be seen by a rape trauma team that can assess injury and administer both medical attention and the psychological care necessary to treat the emotional crisis in the aftermath of the attack. Even under reasonably good circumstances, a medical exam following a rape can be difficult for a victim who has already been traumatized.

First, since her condition is typically not life-threatening, she is likely to be kept waiting in an emergency room for as long as it takes for her to be seen, perhaps several hours. Gunshot wounds, automobile accidents, heart attacks and other life-threatening illnesses and injuries are always seen first. The rape victim may also not be informed that the exam entails the gathering of physical evidence ultimately needed by the prosecution. This need for extensive evidence is usually not readily apparent to the victim of sexual assault.

The physical exam includes not only a gynecological exam (uncomfortable under the best of circumstances), but also a search of the victim's body for physical evidence of the assailant including hairs, fibers, semen and blood. The examiner also searches for evidence of trauma including cuts, bruises and other evidence of force or penetration. Photographs may be taken. In short, the physical exam is both invasive and humiliating, making the rape survivor feel once again abused and victimized.

In addition to the physical exam, a rape survivor will doubtless be subjected to endless questions which require her to relive the attack in vivid detail. She is likely to be asked in intimate detail about her medical history, previous and recent sexual activity, use of contraception and the specific, graphic details of the assault. She will probably be queried about her own drug and alcohol use, particularly during the evening of the assault. Blood and urine specimens may be requested.

In short, the stop for medical assessment and attention is invasive. It violates the victim's privacy and is often physically painful — all at a time when she has already been severely traumatized, manipulated and overcome by a crisis that prevents her from thinking clearly and rationally. Despite her pain and upset, despite her confusion, disorientation and possible incoherence, she is interrogated about her personal history, experiences and habits, and will be repeatedly asked to describe the traumatic details of the attack, something she has already done for the police.

The Third Stop: The Prosecutor

To prosecute an accused rapist, the police must be convinced that the complaint has merit. The police will almost always be willing to take a report, but whether a complaint will reach the district attorney's office (the prosecutor) is usually a matter of police discretion. When the complaint reaches the district attorney's office, the legal hurdles begin.

At the outset it is important to realize that a prosecutor will only want to pursue a case with a strong chance of conviction. The district attorney has to justify the time and expense of prosecuting a case. Near misses don't count. Hence, the prosecutor will go to great lengths to verify the victim's story, to search for inconsistencies and to evaluate the victim as a witness, including finding out what kind of background might be revealed.

Cases of date rape are particularly problematic in this regard. If there was a prior relationship, particularly if consensual sex had occurred in the past, a prosecutor will feel obligated to "grill" a victim (as the defense counsel will) to determine if she will remain credible. Particularly in cases of acquaintances, the nature of the relationship between the victim and the assailant will be of great importance to the prosecutor who can expect the defense to use — indeed exploit — that relationship to cast doubt on the credibility of the victim.

Step three requires a rape victim, who is already probably feeling little sympathy and compassion from the system that she thought would protect her, to be willing to cooperate with the prosecution by enduring its inquiries. Often the vigor of the process that the prosecution needs to win its case leaves the victim, whom it's supposed to serve, feeling cold and betrayed. It requires remarkable stamina and courage to pursue each phase of the process in order to bring a case to "justice."

The Fourth Stop: Mental Health Counseling

Even if the medical and legal intervention that a victim encounters leaves her feeling cold and dissatisfied, she might still expect that those who are entrusted with her emotional well-being will be more sensitive to her needs. One problem sometimes arises from the fact that rape crisis personnel are often volunteers with little training to deal with the complexity of the reactions of rape victims. Indeed, many are rape survivors themselves and, without being trained professionals in this field, may inadvertently overidentify with the victim's experience, possibly very different from that of another victim. Yet, unless a victim can find and afford a mental health professional trained to deal with sexual assault, a volunteer may be the only available mental health intervention that she gets. Some communities have rape crime victims' compensation boards that help defray the costs of medical and psychological assistance.

Another shortcoming of the rape crisis system is that the staff may be competent to deal with the victim, but unprepared to address the whole picture, such as the victim's partner or family, who have themselves been profoundly affected by the rape and who also influence the victim's recovery. Again, many of the staff, which consists of volunteers or poorly trained individuals, may have little understanding of the full set of dynamics that confront a rape victim.

Finally, many rape victims do not seek professional assistance at all, even rape crisis personnel, but instead rely on family and friends to get them through the crisis. While some undoubtedly provide good emotional support and are a good source of needed strength, others may be well-meaning but simply unable to deal with this type of trauma. They may themselves be reacting to the effects of the rape on their own lives and be incapable of providing supportive intervention to result in a positive healing experience. The victim and her family may not even realize that their needs are not being addressed and consequently may not reach out to those who can help. Thus even the mental health community, from which the rape victim would expect the greatest empathy and compassion, may leave her feeling frustrated and disappointed because, although well-intentioned, it is simply not equipped to offer meaningful help.

CINDY'S STORY

I moved to Chicago last summer because my company, a large advertising firm, was seeing hard times and was consolidating some of its branch offices. I had two choices: Move to a major city or stand in an unemployment line. The economy was so bad that, even as one of the company's top sales associates, I had no guarantee that I could find another job. I really had no choice — I had to move.

I grew up in a small town outside Durham, North Carolina, and moving to Chicago for me was as foreign as moving from Boise, Idaho, to Morocco. I was used to safe streets, friendly people and everybody in town knowing everyone else. I had no idea what it was like to be in a big city, except that I soon got an education I would never forget.

I moved into a one-bedroom apartment in a high-rise building about two miles from my new office and just outside of the downtown area. I didn't know a soul and was pleased when a man named Tom, who lived on my floor, befriended me. He never really talked much, but we would smile and exchange pleasantries. He was older than me, probably in his late forties. I was 26. I have to admit, though, that I thought he was attractive, and I was flattered that he seemed to notice me.

About a month after I moved in, I began to sense that Tom seemed to be watching me. I would see him several days in a row as I would leave or return from work. He'd either be standing at the elevator or hanging out in the hall with a newspaper or something in his hand. At first I didn't make much of it, but eventually it seemed strange that we would cross paths so often. This went on for several weeks, and I was both puzzled and flattered by his casual comments, all that we ever exchanged. He would admire my dress, my hair or just the fact that I acted pleasant, and he would go on his way.

The night that it all happened, I had come home from work late, probably about 8:30 p.m. I had not run into Tom, but about a half hour after I got in, there was a tap on my door. It was Tom. He explained that his telephone was out of order and asked if he could use mine. I was just getting undressed so I let him into the living room (where the phone was), and I went back into the bedroom to finish what I was doing. In retrospect that was probably very stupid. I had a strange man in my apartment, and there I was getting undressed.

After about three minutes, I was almost completely undressed and reaching for a nightgown when my bedroom door opened and Tom entered, closing it behind him. He wasn't a bit embarrassed about finding me undressed, but walked over to me calmly and deliberately. I was shocked. I didn't know whether to scream or to order him out. In any event, I never got a chance to do either before he put one of his hands over my mouth and ran his other hand over my partially naked body. I started to push him away, but he was much stronger than I. He squeezed my face so tight that at one point I thought he was going to choke me. He threw me on the bed, face down. I couldn't see him, but I could hear his heavy breathing and feel his hands moving over me. No one is ever prepared for something like this and certainly not a small town girl like me.

I was terrified and on the edge of panic when all of a sudden Tom's calm manner changed, and he seemed to become nervous and agitated. He began to talk to me in an angry way. He said that I had flirted, and he knew I was a tease by the way I dressed for him and smiled at him, leading him on, and that this is what "girls" get when they "act like bitches." Then he violently rolled me onto my back and put one hand over my mouth and throat while he proceeded to undo his own pants. He pried my legs apart and forced himself into me. I was so terrorized that I can feel myself starting to shake even now as I tell the story over again.

We had intercourse, and after only a few seconds, it was over. The whole episode only lasted a matter of minutes. Then the strangest thing happened. He seemed comfortably relaxed, even concerned about me and asked if I was okay. Okay? He's got to be kidding! It was as though he wanted me to forget what had happened and pretend that I had just had a great time. Throughout the whole horrible thing I had not uttered a sound. I was so

scared and stunned that it felt like my mind had
left my body, as though the violence was happening to someone else.

What Happened?

Cindy was a victim of classic acquaintance rape.
She knew her assailant and allowed him into her
home without giving it a second thought because
he was familiar, and familiarity is too often equat-
ed with trust. Her upbringing in a small rural
town where people felt secure because everyone
knew everyone else did not prepare her for the
realities of a big city environment. She failed to
take even the most basic precautions by allowing
this essentially unknown man into her apartment.

Cindy immediately moved out of her apartment
and stayed with a friend until she could find another place to live. Even then, however, her work
life and social life were disrupted and her atten-
dance at the job became so sporadic and unpredictable that eventually she was dismissed. She
never did receive any help in dealing with this
episode, and the only person she ever told was the
friend with whom she went to live.

Rape trauma syndrome affects all victims, although the symptoms they manifest may be markedly different. In this case, Cindy chose not to acknowledge and confront the trauma, and her ability
to recover from it is likely to be negatively affected
by that choice. In any event, if she does eventually
decide to prosecute her assailant, her use of rape
trauma syndrome as evidence of the crime will not
only assist in determining that the rape happened,
but will also help explain why victims do not always
report the incident immediately, if at all.

This was not a dating situation, and clearly Cindy did nothing wrong that would have provoked this attack. The acquaintance relationship would make her case more difficult to prove in court if her assailant were indicted and the case got that far. In fact, Cindy never even reported the crime. Many victims of acquaintance rape never do. They are either frightened by the assailant, who threatens to harm them if they report the crime, or they are deterred by the law enforcement personnel who are very reluctant to prosecute acquaintance rape because of the difficulty in obtaining a conviction, assuming, of course, that they even believe the victim. Cindy might have had a strong case since in her situation there was no alcohol present and the parties had never dated each other. These factors can aid a prosecution if the victim has the courage to risk coming forward.

CHAPTER TWO

The Rapists: Who They Are, Why They Rape And How To Avoid Them

Who are the rapists? How do you identify them? Why do men become rapists and what can potential targets do to minimize the likelihood of being victimized?

The answers to these questions are not simple. "Typical" rapists can be described on the basis of demographic information, such as how old they are or how wealthy. Their psychological makeup and their personalities can be described. But when all is said and done, what we find is that most males who commit acquaintance rape appear to be indistinguishable from any other men. In other words, rapists come from all walks of life and most have very few separate, special or identifiable personality patterns. Yet it is because they are so difficult to identify

that it is important to know who they are — their profiles
and warning signs — to avoid being victimized.

Profile Of A Rapist

Statistics of reported rapes profile a "typical" rapist
and, although imperfect because of the low rate of reporting, they do provide some useful information. National
crime reports indicate that the greatest concentration of
offenders (over 60%) fall in an age range between 16 and
24 years. The raw numbers indicate that there are nearly
as many black offenders as white offenders, and that low
socioeconomic status is of greater significance than racial
or minority identity.

One theory about criminal behavior maintains that a
"subculture of violence" exists, which includes the poor,
the lower classes, the disenfranchised, the down-and-out
and generally those whose value and belief systems run
counter to those held by the dominant culture. Because
members of this subculture feel both angry and out of
control, they are quick to resort to physical aggression.
Indeed this becomes their way of life, and they resort to
all types of violence, not just rape, when they're unable to
get what they want from the dominant culture. Young
males particularly are taught through example to display
aggression and violence in this way.

Regardless of one's belief in the "subculture" theory, it
is undeniable that most violent acts are perpetrated by
members of the disenfranchised, those who feel little control over their own destinies, related in part to their continued oppression throughout history. Most are either
unskilled workers or unemployed. Most come from an
inner-city population and, incidentally, most victims come
from the same population. Statistics indicate that the incidence of inter-racial rapes is actually quite small, indicating that rape is not particularly a racial issue.

If asked to visualize an image of the typical rapist, most people identify a sadistic, psychopathic or psychotic personality who hates women and expresses this hostility with sexual violence. Yet there is a significant body of evidence to suggest that a rapist can be *any* hostile aggressive male who, usually after drinking, finds himself in a position to do violence to a woman. In fact, after observing individual perpetrators who fit both descriptions, researchers noted that there are at least two types of rapists: a small percentage of rapists act out a deep psychological disturbance expressed through sexual violence, but a greater number of rapists have a psychological makeup that is not much different from the average male, except that certain personal variables (discussed later) lead them to act out a hostility toward women in a sexually deviant way.

There is substantial evidence that most rapists demonstrate no overt psychiatric pathology except for the tendency to rape. In other words, there is no identifiable "rapist" mental disease that consistently separates those who engage in criminal activity from those who commit other violent crimes. The view that all rapists are psychopaths, schizophrenics or other psychotic personalities is simply not borne out by the evidence. Probably the most certain attribute of the "typical" rapist is his propensity to rape repeatedly, often many times.

Many rapists are young, many still in their teens. Rarely do they commit a single, unplanned or unanticipated incident. Indeed every rape begins in the mind of the rapist, where sexual aggression is desired and planned. This is contrary to the traditional image of the rapist as a sexual pervert who flies out of control and does not really know what he is doing. He is, in fact, a male who often has a strong need to control, abuse and degrade women. He is an individual capable of violence and whose violence is expressed sexually. With no identifiable "rapist" personality, it is virtually impossible to recognize and identify a potential offender before his act.

Profile Of A Rape Situation

Contrary to another popular belief, most rapes are apparently planned in advance, either by a single perpetrator or a group of men. In many cases a particular victim is targeted, the victim and the perpetrator are known to each other, and the plan is geared toward luring her into an advantageous situation where they are unlikely to be detected. These are usually the "acquaintance" rape cases. The targeted victim is selected with sexual domination in mind. Violence is the means selected to achieve domination, and the rape is precipitated on the basis of a perceived injustice for which she is held responsible and accountable.

By contrast, in cases of stranger rape, the act but not the victim is usually planned in advance. The victim may be stalked or she may be whoever comes along at the time and fits into the rapist's prearranged plan. The presence of a plan not only increases a perpetrator's ability to complete the rape, but also indicates that he intends to commit this specific crime — that it is not a random act of violence.

A smaller number of rapes, perhaps 25%, are spontaneous in that the offender neither planned nor intended to commit the act at that time. In these cases the perpetrator may have been drinking. He may also have been in the process of committing another crime when the opportunity to rape arose.

- Mark was in the process of committing a burglary on a home which he had "cased" for several hours and assumed was unoccupied. He made his entry through a ground-floor window, only to be encountered by Susan, who was "house-sitting" while the owners were away. When Mark realized that Susan was so terrified of him that he could make her do whatever he wanted, the idea of raping her came to him. With Susan too petrified to resist, the rape was accomplished with little struggle. It is often the rapist's experience of complete power and control over his victim and her absolute fear of him that stimulate him and lead him to commit the rape.

Most rapists make their attacks between 8 p.m. and 2 a.m. More rapes occur on weekends than on weekdays, and more rapes occur in the warmer months. In addition, the presence of alcohol or drugs is likely. However, the "typical" rapist is not drunk but has been drinking enough to significantly lower his inhibitions.

The presence of force, especially the use of a weapon is usually associated with stranger rape. In this type of rape, the great majority of single perpetrators carry some sort of weapon, particularly if the rape occurs where a would-be victim might try to escape or call for help. If the attack occurs in the victim's home or car, there is less need for a weapon. Similarly, as the number of offenders increases, as in gang rape, the need for a weapon decreases.

In cases of acquaintance relationships where the offender can lure a victim into a private spot, such as his or her home, there is usually little need for a weapon. When a weapon is used, it is primarily to overcome any resistance on the part of the victim.

Some Theories On Why Men Become Rapists

Psychological Theories

Much of the way we view sexual aggression has been influenced by the theories of Sigmund Freud. Freud contributed significantly to the understanding of internal psychological processes and their relationship to external reality. His basic focus was on internal psychological conflicts and drives. In his early work he wrote extensively about what he believed to be man's basic drives: sex and aggression. Although Freud himself wrote nothing about the act of rape, his followers have applied his theories to understanding the bizarre act of rape.

According to Freudian "psychodynamic" theory, a rapist probably suffers from an internal conflict created by a clash of his own normal drives and the sanctions, prohibitions and controls placed on him by his own parents, particularly his mother. The mother is the central figure in Freudian theory. If a boy grows up with a mother who is demanding, dominating and punitive, and who is distant and rejecting, he becomes "fixated" at an early stage of his emotional development. This is a stage in which the conflict is dominated by issues of power, aggression and control.

Freud postulated that when a young boy's natural erotic attraction to his mother is thwarted by her cold rejecting nature, he becomes frustrated and enraged, then his sexual and aggressive drives become enmeshed so that love and hate become indistinguishable. He develops an intense desire to dominate, control and even humiliate women who symbolize his anger toward the person who treated him this way — his mother. In some men the ability to dominate, terrify and control a woman leads to intense sexual excitement and becomes a necessary component for sexual release and satisfaction.

The motivations of the rapist may also stem from feelings of sexual inadequacy and the need to defend himself against his own dependency needs. He never managed to resolve these while growing up because his mother kept him powerless and inadequate as a male figure. At the same time there is often no male figure to balance the influence of the mother and help the boy identify, develop and express his masculinity and aggression through acceptable channels. Such a male becomes a "sexual psychopath" (a favorite Freudian term) whose unconscious sexual desires stem from his own feelings of inadequacy expressed through anger and a need to control others, particularly women.

Other theorists who have studied men who rape have developed ideas based more on their observations than on theoretical formulations. These theorists describe two basic types of rapists.

First, there are those men who view their mothers, and women in general, as sacred, virtuous and model individuals. Since childhood they have thought of their mothers in positive, glowing terms and have thus overidealized this female. So strong is this overidealization that these men see themselves in relation to this image as inferior and inadequate. Over time these men invest women (symbolizing mother) with tremendous power over their own feelings. As women become more powerful, they, as men, become weaker. When they must deal with the inevitable rejections that occur in life, their reactions are exaggerated and their sense of inferiority becomes profound. These feelings can become so strong and painful that they have to be pushed out of conscious awareness, leaving the man vulnerable to dealing with frustrations through aggression and hostility. Because his aggression and hostility are directed toward the source of frustration — women — then violating, humiliating and dirtying a woman is a way for him to elevate his own self-esteem. Motivated by hate and revenge, he feels more adequate and superior harming a woman. To feel good about himself, he needs to put a woman down. If he succeeds without getting caught, he will probably rape again and again. He feels little remorse for his act.

The second type of rapist described by these theorists is the man who actually believes that women are "asking for it" regardless of what they say. This man can interpret any behavior on the part of a woman as an invitation for sex. How a woman dresses, where she goes, who she is friendly with, how she talks or almost any behavior is interpreted as "asking for it." These men seem to be dealing with an overwhelming impulse that they cannot resist. If apprehended, they may be contrite and regret their loss of legal and moral perspective. Some do experience feelings of sorrow for the harmful acts they commit, although many contend that they would not have forced themselves on the woman had they not been provoked or teased.

Sociobiological Theory

Other researchers have sought an explanation for sexually aggressive male behavior that relates to male and female reproductive instincts. The sexual drive in both men and women is doubtlessly related to reproduction of the species. The question is whether sexual violence is some sort of extension of the natural male sex drive or whether deviance is too aberrant to flow logically from natural reproductive processes.

In virtually all animal species, including human beings, the role of the male is to mate in order to fertilize an embryo produced by the female. It is also the role of the female to mate, but only with a select male. This both reproduces the species and upgrades the gene pool, improving the species with each succeeding generation. But while the male's natural role is to fertilize as many embryos as possible, the female goes through a reproductive cycle and can mate only at certain times. Thus her natural role is to provide viable embryos, to have those embryos fertilized by high-order males, who will produce high quality offspring, and then to nurture and rear those offspring to maturity. (The definition of an improved "genetic pool" and "high-order male" varies from species to species.)

Given this normal biological scheme, it is expected that males will continuously try to have sexual intercourse with receptive and fertile females, while females will be far more selective in their mating choices and will nest and nurture rather than roam. The male, not hampered by fertility cycles, has a continuous sex drive and is always looking for receptive females.

Assuming that human beings have similar biological and sexual drives, theorists speculate that a man's relationships with women will be highly sexualized and he will, as he matures, be required to learn the species and cultural rules regarding the gratification of his sexual drives. He must also learn that sexual needs may be less intense in females and a woman is likely to be more protective of her sexuality. At the same time, the cultural rules concerning sexual availability of women are usually taught to boys by women (e.g., mothers, sisters, teachers). When this education takes place in a caring and supportive nest, the harsh realities of "don't touch" and "not now" are tempered by the love within the family arrangement. In a hurtful, shaming and punishing environment, the young man's sexual development is severely damaged. He does not accept the rules of his culture, but learns to express his feelings of humiliation, pain and rage in an arbitrary and vengeful fashion.

How is this model useful to understanding the psychology of the rapist? First, it starts with an understanding of normal human sexuality and male/female differences. Second, sexual offenders probably fall along a continuum, ranging from seemingly normal males gone astray to those who engage in repetitive, violent and pathological sexual deviance. Some of these men force themselves on women because they have not come to understand that "no" always means "no." They only coerce a woman into having sex under specific circumstances (e.g., after drug or alcohol use, or under peer pressure). For some, this loss of control may occur only once. Furthermore, their goal is usually not to physically harm the woman, but only to satisfy their sexual drive. At a further point along the continuum are those men who, after engaging in such behavior and having their needs met with no other consequences, start thinking that "no" really means "yes." They go on to repeat the act again, believing that sexual coercion is just part of normal and expected male and female interactions.

Yet further along the continuum are men who engage in repetitive, violent behavior that is expressed through sexual deviance. These men closely resemble others who are violent and antisocial in other nonsexual ways. Their emotional and sexual development likely has been severely disrupted, usually in childhood. Often they have been physically and sexually abused themselves.

The sociobiological model urges that evolution requires the male to be sexually aggressive and predisposes him to sexualize relationships with females in order to perform his biological function. When significant psychological issues are present, such as child or sexual abuse, some men act out their pain and anger, particularly if it is directed at a woman through sexual aggression. Viewed this way, rape would be on the extreme end of the continuum which ranges from male sexual attraction, to various forms of sexual coercion and transgression, and finally to serial sexual aggression and violence. According to this model, even the most violent rapes fall along the behavioral continuum and even significant deviation can be explained without reference to specific psychiatric disorders or mental disease.

Feminist Theory

Feminist theory accepts the basic premise that there are biologically-based male/female differences and does not reject the idea that there may be a continuum from sexual attraction to coercion to aggression. However, it focuses on the effects of cultural socialization patterns (e.g., status, power, financial resources and control of cultural institutions, such as police or courts) on the male desire to exploit his biological evolution (e.g., physical size, strength or energy) to gratify his innate sexual desires. The feminist model contends that there is a cultural component to the evolutionary process. Most cultures are headed by men and value male supremacy and domination, thus sanctioning male values of competition and aggression. This allows and even encourages men to act on their primitive impulses. It teaches them that using force to prevail is masculine and using coercion and other abusive behavior toward women is an acceptable way of expressing anger, frustration and the need for control and dominance. This sanction of force stops short, of course, of allowing sexual violence, but it gives males mixed signals about their relationships with women. These cultures provide men with an image of women as sexual objects. Men are seen as superior, having the right to dominate women. Cultural sanctions allow men to degrade and exploit women, promoting the use and even abuse of women. Indeed, women who have been targets of outright violence such as stalking, battering or rape have found that the male-dominated criminal justice and medical systems are ambivalent about their roles in assisting victimized women.

Violence Theory

Researchers and theorists have long debated the question of whether the dominant motivation of rapists is to express anger and aggression through physical violence or, alternatively, whether the act of rape has at its roots a primarily sexual motive. Like the question of whether there is a specific rapist pathology, the answer is probably that there are different kinds of rapists whose motivations are as varied as their personalities. One way of approaching this issue is to look at the various types of acts and consider each on its own.

The Aggressive Model

In some cases the rape victim is not only assaulted for the purpose of rape, but she is also brutally beaten, mutilated or even killed. Here the rapist is not satisfied by merely raping her but also needs to dirty, humiliate or otherwise degrade the victim. Usually the victim of this

type of rapist is a stranger and the intensity and vicious-
ness of the attack suggests that the expression of anger is
its primary purpose. Clinicians speculate that such offenders feel intense rage toward one or more specific
women (e.g., mothers, sisters, grandmothers or teachers)
and simply "displace" their desire to hurt or humiliate
these specific women by assaulting anyone who happens
along, fits the image and is vulnerable to abuse.

Offenders who demonstrate this violent and brutal
pattern usually attack a number of victims, but may otherwise have a relatively normal life and psychological
history. In studies, these men usually appear to have an
active and seemingly normal sex life. In reality, however,
they have troubled heterosexual relationships that are
marked by domestic conflict and often violence. Such
men are likely to view women as hostile and demanding,
as well as cold and withholding, justifying their anger
and violence. They may have relatively normal social and
employment backgrounds and otherwise present themselves as adequately adjusted people. A small number
are, indeed, genuine psychopaths and antisocial personalities. Yet whether they are diagnosed as psychopathic
rapists or rapists whose personalities are not much different than others, these men cannot deal with women as
equals, sex partners or even as human beings.

The Sexual Model

Another group of offenders display characteristics in
which the motivations for the rape appear to be primarily
sexual. The most obvious distinction from the aggressive
model is that the behavior is coercive but it is usually not
violent and evidence of brutality is absent. Force is used
only to accomplish the rape act, during which the victim
may be gagged or restrained from escaping. Otherwise
she is usually left physically unharmed. In fact, the offender may even act kindly after the rape. Moreover, if

too much force is necessary to counter the victim's resistance, he may release her and allow her to flee.

The primary purpose of this type of act is to satisfy the rapist's sexual need. The rape act is motivated by sexual wishes or fantasies, and the rapist is able to perform and achieve satisfaction under these coercive circumstances. In fact, he has probably rehearsed the act many times in his fantasy, indicating that his behavior is not the result of an overwhelming impulse but is carefully planned. The nature of the act lacks any sadistic quality. Its primary intent is sexual pleasure. The most significant attribute of this type of offender is that he exhibits little or no other antisocial behavior. He may appear to others as a loner, isolated from most social contact. Except for his repeated sexual offenses, he may display little other hostile, aggressive or even particularly assertive behavior.

The Sexual Aggressive Model

Still a third category of offenders falls into a group in which the motivations for rape appear to be both sexual and aggressive. These offenders exhibit characteristics of both models, forming a third identifiable pattern. Here the behavior appears to be geared toward generating sexual excitement that is unattainable without the presence of some type of violence. The rapist uses violence to arouse himself sexually, but after committing the offense, no further aggression is displayed. Interestingly, research shows that this type of aggression is not accompanied by an outward display of anger, although underlying feelings of anger probably still drive the aggression. There may also be some component of sadism in that the violence is necessary to generate sexual excitement.

The personal relationships of this type of rapist indicate that there may be a specific, identifiable pathology present. The offender is both hostile and aggressive in most interpersonal situations and demonstrates little sense of affection, compassion or empathy. He may be married but is more likely to have been divorced at least once. His sexual needs, driven by an overwhelming need for aggressive seduction, make it unlikely that he can sustain a marital relationship. The psychological history of such a rapist is characterized by antisocial behavior and little effort is made to conform to social norms. As he strives to satisfy his own needs by coercing and exploiting others, aggression plays a large part in fulfilling his sexual needs.

Group Or Gang Rape

Nearly half of all rapes appear to be perpetrated by at least two men together, dispelling the common belief that most rapists are secretive, individual offenders who jump out of the bushes, commit their offenses and immediately disappear. Working at least in pairs not only increases the odds of completing the act without detection, but also allows a male to demonstrate to another male the power, control and dominance that is apparently at the root of most violent sexual group activity. Group rape consists of two or more people who act together to perpetrate the rape offense, even if not every participant performs a sexual act during the rape. Gang rape usually refers to more than three offenders who commit rape to prove their masculinity to each other. This motive provides an additionally powerful incentive when added to those motivations discussed earlier in the various rapist descriptions.

Gang or group rape is often initiated on a dare and can be even more vicious and brutal than rape by a sole perpetrator. This is true, if for no other reason than the obvious physical advantage and the victim's lack of opportunity to resist. The intent is often not only to have sex with the woman but also to abuse and humiliate her by making her an object of contempt and for the men to prove themselves to each other.

The psychology of such a group appears to reflect a distortion of the phenomenon known as "male bonding." In normal male bonding, men identify with one another to strengthen and demonstrate their masculinity and power. When this process is distorted, as in gang rape, the men act out their own internal conflicts and unresolved psychological issues. The group's acting in concert gives each member the opportunity to prove to the others both his ability to commit the rape act and his allegiance to the group. The males are allied together against the victim, which can occur even though the men are not acquainted with each other. The bonding results whether the offenders are members of an organized gang or have simply gathered together for an evening, perhaps with no planned intent to commit a rape. The group activity itself creates opportunity for male bonding to occur. The group works together to plan and execute an offense coordinating such tasks as securing the location and "taking turns" to commit the rape. Thus the significant experience for the gang participant is largely that of the relationship between himself and the other offenders, while the rape itself may be almost incidental.

Implications For The Victim:
How To Avoid Potential Rapists

From these theories and ideas, one can see that there is no way to tell if a man is a rapist from his conversation or appearance. Most rapists look and sound like other men. Most exhibit the same range of physical, personality and sociocultural characteristics found in the general population of men. The rapist is not a glassy-eyed, foaming-at-the mouth lunatic or monster. He ultimately distinguishes himself from other men by the very act of rape itself.

If one cannot distinguish a rapist from any other male until after he rapes, can a woman do anything to minimize the possibility of sexual assault? The answer may depend on the type of rape being planned. There may be little that a woman can do to prevent a rape by a stranger under any circumstances. Nevertheless, since most rapes are committed by men known to their victims, there are a number of things a woman can do to reduce the possibility of becoming a victim of date or acquaintance rape.

Guidelines To Prevent Rape

1. Stay away from men who do not treat women respectfully. This is not always easy to identify since a man who is trying to gain a woman's confidence will usually try to conduct himself properly. A woman cannot know what is going on in his mind. She should be aware that male/female encounters have a strong sexual dynamic, particularly from the perspective of the male. If her interest in sex is not the same as his, there will be conflicting sexual tensions inherent in the relationship. This can provide the motivation for coercive behavior on the male's part. If a man makes a woman feel uncomfortable, she should trust her intuition and act to promote her safety.

2. Avoid men who exploit others, men or women. Men who exploit others in nondating or nonsexual situations are likely to exploit women in sexually-charged situations. If a man treats other people as objects to do his bidding or sees women as being inferior and in service to men, he may expect and demand sexual favors regardless of what the woman wants.

3. Avoid men who disregard laws and established rules. Men who knowingly break laws and behave without regard for the rights of others are at risk for doing the same sexually. If they want

sex, they may take it without thought for their partners.

4. Avoid situations that could become dangerous. Once again, it is not always easy to anticipate which situations could turn ugly, but these general principles, if followed, will tend to reduce the risk of being involved in an unwanted sexual encounter.

   a. Avoid being in an isolated place with a man who is not well known. If a woman allows herself to go to an isolated place, the man may believe that she is as interested in sex as he is. Also, being isolated severely limits a woman's options to call for help or get away if needed.

   b. Avoid being with a man in places where there is a lot of male peer pressure, such as a men's dormitory, fraternity house or social club. A man who is seemingly nice and respectful when alone with a woman may feel pressure to prove himself when he is around his buddies and his reputation for male prowess is on the line. This could also be a setup for a gang rape situation.

   c. Avoid being totally dependent on a date for transportation. Make alternative arrangements with a friend or have money for a cab or bus. A woman should never allow herself to become totally dependent until she knows the man very well. Double-dating is also helpful in this regard.

5. Avoid allowing a man to touch or get too close before the relationship has developed very far. If a woman feels uncomfortable and that her boundaries are being violated, she should tell the man in no uncertain terms that his behavior is unacceptable. This is very important. Personal boundary violations are a first sign of an impending problem. Take action immediately.

6. Avoid using alcohol or drugs with a man who is not well known. Alcohol or drug use is all too common in many acquaintance rape situations. Alcohol lowers inhibitions and impairs judgment. If a woman is herself intoxicated, her ability to deal with a difficult situation is impaired. Unless a woman knows a man well, she is not safe in the presence of drug or alcohol abuse. She should not stay with a man she does not know well who is becoming intoxicated.

The more information that a woman has about rapists and the conditions that invite or promote sexual violence, the more she can do to reduce the likelihood of becoming a rape victim. Rape has occurred throughout the ages and no doubt will continue as a part of the human drama. Despite this, women will continue to date and to seek meaningful connections with men. Knowing the dangers, reading the warning signs and being able to take appropriate action if necessary enable women to enjoy dating with less fear of being abused.

DEBBIE'S STORY

Telling my story has never been easy for me. Even after years of counseling, I still get very emotional and have to work to hold back the tears. I'm 37 years old now and should be at a pretty solid place in my life. People who don't know me well would probably think I am. They see only the outside.

I live in a nice house in an up-scale suburban town. I have a good husband and a terrific eight-year-old daughter. I have a college degree, and I work as a free-lance editor. Look good? Yes. Feel good? Not really. The fact is that I work free-lance because I have not been able to hold down a job. I always seem to have a run-in with a supervisor, make a major blunder or get really ticked off or upset about something. The longest I've been able to stay on the job is nine months. I also like working at home where I can sort of keep an eye on my daughter. I'm probably over-protective of her, but I just can't help it. I don't feel that the world is a safe place, even in my nice house in a nice town.

My husband is a terrific guy. He makes a good living and is interesting and very supportive. He's had to put up with an awful lot from me, but he has stuck it out even through times when I've done everything I could to push him away. He complains about our lack of intimacy. He says it really bothers him that I want to sleep all the time, that I get sick a lot and that I have little interest in sex. I used to be really defensive about these things — especially sex — and would say things to hurt him just to keep him away and then make him feel that it was his fault. I was also afraid of losing him. I guess it's a good sign that I don't do that anymore. I'm more willing to admit my problems now, but I'm still pretty numb as far as my feelings are concerned. I'm really lucky that he's still here. He truly deserves better.

I still haven't told you what happened. This is because I have to work my way up to telling my story.

I grew up in a fairly well-to-do family. My father was a successful businessman and my mother was a professional woman. They gave me lots of material things. I could actually have pretty much anything money could buy. My parents were al-ways busy, either working or out to one social affair or another. They didn't enjoy being around kids and used money as a substitute for their love and time. We always had servants to do all the things they didn't like doing, like taking care of me. Ever since I can remember, they had a mar-ried couple who lived in. Betty's job was to take care of me, the house and the laundry. Frank, her husband, took care of the grounds, cars and house repairs. When I turned 11, he began to take care of me, too.

Things might have happened before that, but I don't have any clear memories before I was 11. Until the last few years, I was not even clear about that. But now I know what happened. I remember coming home from school one day in May. The weather was warm and I was looking forward to going out to play. I went up to my room to change my school clothes. I had taken everything off except my underwear and was standing in front of the mirror, when I spotted Frank's reflection. He was peeking at me through the partly open door, and he was rubbing his crotch. He had a strange excited look in his eyes. Our eyes met in the mirror and he ducked away and left. I was stunned. Even though I didn't know what he was doing, I knew that something was wrong and I felt scared. I didn't know what to do. My parents were rarely around. I knew that if I went to them about what had happened, they would probably say that I was imagining things because I watched the wrong things on TV and probably ground me for my own good. I decided to keep my mouth shut, forget about what I saw and act like nothing had happened. In fact, nothing more did happen right away. As a couple of weeks went by, I began to wonder if I had really imagined it all.

Summer was coming and I was looking forward to going away to camp. One afternoon Betty was out shopping and I was watching TV. Frank came into the room and sat down next to me. He said he wanted to talk to me about what had happened a couple of weeks before. He told me that it was good that I hadn't told anyone. He said that my parents didn't really care about me since they never spent any time with me, and Betty wouldn't believe me and would only get angry with me for telling tales. He told me that he really cared for me. He watched me grow up, he said, and felt like I was the prettiest girl he had ever known. He felt as if I belonged to him and that he was responsible for caring for me and teaching me about life. He began to touch me, first on the arm and then on my chest and legs. He seemed to be getting very excited and got that look in his eyes again.

Then he did what I had never even imagined before. He opened his pants and took out his penis and began to rub it fast. It looked huge, and I was so shocked and frightened that I literally froze. I tried to yell for him to stop, but nothing came out of my mouth. I just sat there as if I were in a trance. He finished in a few minutes, but it felt like a lifetime to me. Time seemed to stand still. Frank told me not to tell anyone or I would get into trouble and my summer plans would be ruined. He said it would be our secret and that he would teach me about the "birds and the bees." I was in shock but nodded okay.

That night, after Betty had gone to bed and my parents were out for a late evening, Frank came into my room and began giving me an "education" that I would never forget. Without going into too much graphic detail, since it still upsets me so much, Frank went from fondling himself to forcing me to have sexual intercourse with him. I tried to push him away but he was so strong, I didn't have a chance. He forced himself on me every chance he could which was every time we were alone. Initially, after each time, he would both reassure me and threaten me. Eventually, however, he would just give me a look and leave. This went on until I went away to camp and started up again when I came home. A couple of times I approached my parents and tried to tell them, but they were so impatient with me that I just gave up. My whole life had changed. I couldn't concentrate on anything and felt depressed most of the time. I always felt lonely but was afraid of being with people. I had few friends and boys thought I was weird and stayed away. Sometimes I could overhear them making fun of me.

Frank sexually abused me until I was 14 years old. The only reason it stopped was because Betty got sick and they had to move to a warmer climate. My parents finally noticed that something was wrong when I kept doing poorly in school, spent a lot of time alone and generally acted like an angry brat. When I made my first suicide attempt after not getting invited to the junior prom, they sent me to see a shrink. By that time I felt so helpless, angry, depressed and defensive that I could not use the professional help. There were a couple of more suicide attempts over the years, but it wasn't until I met my husband that I had any hope or motivation to work things out. Frank died about ten years ago. If he were still alive I would seriously think about pursuing legal action.

What Happened?

Debbie's story is a clear example of statutory as well as acquaintance rape. She and Frank knew each other over a long period of time and she was originally taught to trust Frank. As is becoming more apparent, this type of sexual abuse often happens to girls under the age of 12, is perpetrated by someone who is known and often trusted and goes on for a long period of time. A variety of sexual acts were forced on Debbie. He used both physical force and psychological coercion to intimidate and overwhelm her. Debbie learned to cope initially by dissociating the experience. As she describes it, she "froze" or no longer had a sense that these things were happening to her. She didn't feel anything.

To cope over the long run, she repressed the experiences. This is essentially a form of psychological forgetting in which the intolerable events are buried so deeply in the person's unconscious that they actually forget what took place. This was not a particularly effective coping mechanism for Debbie since there were so many traumatic events over almost a four-year period. With emotionally detached, self-involved and unresponsive parents, Debbie was essentially left alone to cope. Acts of rape and sexual abuse are acts that do not discriminate. They happen to rich, poor, attractive, lonely, black or white and young as well as old. The effects of such trauma in childhood are profound and long lasting.

Although Debbie acknowledges meeting her husband as the beginning of her recovery, her dysfunction was so deep that, even with his loving patience and other extensive professional help, she was still unable to have normal intimate relationships with him or their child. She has difficulty with relationships at work and performs well below her capabilities.

At the time of this writing, Debbie reports that she is finally beginning to feel the positive effects of the hard work she has been doing to recover from her experiences. She is hopeful and optimistic for the first time in her life. Although she knows she will always be vulnerable and prone to depression and withdrawal from relationships, she says she can spot a potential problem sooner and get through it faster. She has even begun to experience feelings of love, joy and satisfaction.

In Conclusion

This case is an example of typical acquaintance rape demonstrating a number of relevant points and issues. Clearly it does not capture every possible set of situations or circumstances, but it is representative of the broad spectrum of acquaintance-type rape.

CHAPTER THREE

Rape Trauma Syndrome: What It Is And How It Is Used In Court

Virtually every woman who is raped, either by a stranger or by an acquaintance, suffers a significant, dramatic and usually identifiable emotional and physical reaction to the attack. Not every woman reacts in the same way, but many experts on sexual assault have suggested that there is a relationship between the nature of her reaction and her eventual recovery from the trauma.

- Two weeks after being forcibly raped by a man she met at a friend's party, Susan was unable to return to her bedroom where the attack occurred. She continued to break down in tears at any mention of the incident and had frequent nightmares about being killed. She had great difficulty being alone, although she also had little interest in socializing. Susan was unable to return to work for a month and even then could only tolerate working part-time.

• Ten days after she was violated by a rapist, Christine still refused to discuss the attack with even her closest family, friends or a rape crisis counselor. She was embarrassed by the incident and blamed herself for letting it happen and not taking prudent precautions or fighting off her attacker. If not for her initial upset, no one would ever know that anything had happened. Christine appeared calm and controlled and refused to prosecute her rapist.

• Michelle had a good sexual relationship with her husband prior to being raped by another man, but was unable to respond sexually to him even five months after the attack. Her husband blamed himself for not being at home to protect his wife and felt rejected by her sudden lack of interest in him. As their sex life deteriorated, the couple grew apart from each other and they eventually separated.

• Maureen was still plagued by guilt over being forcibly raped despite the passage of two years. She constantly reviewed the incident and how she might have prevented it. She had not been sexually active before the attack, and her fear and confusion — even years later — have prevented her from establishing an intimate relationship. Although she has been willing to go on dates, she has sabotaged any relationship that might lead to a sexual encounter on the grounds that the men would not understand her mixed feelings.

In 1974, an historic study at Boston City Hospital by Ann Burgess and Lynda Holmstrom involved interviews of approximately 100 women admitted to the emergency room after being raped. The researchers studied the short-

and long-term consequences of being raped, and labeled their findings "rape trauma syndrome." They described the various physical, behavioral and emotional reactions that raped women suffer. Subsequent studies have confirmed the Burgess and Holmstrom results and documented an even wider range of reactions of rape victims during various intervals, from hours to years after the attack.

What Is Rape Trauma Syndrome?

Medical authorities consider Rape Trauma Syndrome to be a form of Post-Traumatic Stress Disorder (PTSD) which is a recognized medical diagnosis. Three essential criteria must be present to establish PTSD:

1. The person must suffer a recognizable trauma that would cause distress symptoms in most people.

2. The person must re-experience the trauma through nightmares, flashbacks or recurrent dreams.

3. The person must display decreased involvement with the outside world as demonstrated by at least two of the following:

   a. less interest in significant activities

   b. sleep disturbances

   c. guilt about surviving when others have not

   d. memory loss or trouble concentrating

   e. avoiding activities that are a reminder of the traumatic event

   f. an intensification of symptoms when the victim is exposed to something that resembles the traumatic event.

While the standard diagnostic manual does not specifically identify rape trauma syndrome, it is consistent with the symptoms of PTSD and, therefore, has been recognized as a related syndrome.

Rape trauma syndrome consists of an acute "crisis" phase, a "disorientation" phase and eventually a "reorientation" phase.

Crisis

During the acute crisis phase, which can last from a few hours to several days, victims may be in shock, either displaying virtually no symptoms or (more often) extreme emotional upset with feelings of anger, fear, anxiety, guilt, embarrassment and often disbelief. They frequently report feeling powerless and vulnerable. Physical symptoms include pain, bruising, bleeding, soreness, trembling or shaking, rapid breathing, tight muscles, numbness, loss of appetite and sleep disturbances.

Disorientation

The disorientation phase can follow immediately or can be delayed by several days. During this period, most victims express a wide range of emotions including crying, anger, fear, humiliation, embarrassment, revenge and self-blame. Other victims may react in a much more controlled manner. Their hostile feelings are suppressed, and they appear smiling, calm or restless, without overt signs of distress. Many victims experience nightmares and fears associated with the rape, such as a fear of the dark or places that remind them of the attack. They may question whether the rape really happened or happened as they remember it. They may question their own participation or worry about whether they should or could have resisted. They often limit their activities and may try to suppress their memory of the attack. These women will appear confused, uncertain, inconsistent and may seem to have memory lapses about types of details that most people cannot understand being forgotten.

Reorientation

The reorientation phase, which usually begins two to three weeks after the rape, is substantially affected by a victim's psychological and emotional coping resources. Women with more internal resources will begin to put the event into perspective by "working through" the trauma, which requires understanding the experience and how it affected them. Although the rape cannot be undone, its aftermath can be incorporated into the victim's life, resulting in a constructive recovery. She can gradually regain her confidence and resume her life activities.

Other rape victims never break into the reorientation phase because they repress (involuntarily make unconscious) the effects and the memory of the rape and, therefore, never work through the consequences of the trauma. They may either assume the role of a permanently "helpless victim," or they may appear markedly indifferent, unaffected and carefree. While they avoid situations that trigger the memory of the rape, they also suffer from such aftereffects as nightmares and anxiety for a considerably longer period of time than those who have worked through the trauma.

In both cases victims are likely to change their routines, habits and other behavior. They may change their residences and telephone numbers, they may refuse invitations that require them to be alone or in certain places, and they may either increase or decrease their visits with family and friends. Victims are often more cautious about their lifestyles and may always be more careful about being in circumstances that could result in another attack.

Most victims also experience a significant change, both short- and long-term, in the way they react to a sexual partner. A woman who had not previously been sexually active may experience great difficulty in establishing a normal or healthy sexual relationship for a long time after the rape. A woman who was sexually active prior to the rape is likely to have that relationship disrupted, although it will probably be easier for her to re-establish a satisfactory relationship eventually. Finally the partners of rape victims may also be victimized by the rape. Not only are they concerned about the consequences of the trauma on their partner, but also they often assume some blame and may themselves feel violated by the attack. Such feelings are usually unpredictable and highly disruptive to the existing relationship.

Since the original study by Burgess and Holmstrom, many psychological studies have documented the severity of the trauma caused by rape. It has been demonstrated that several months after a rape, a majority of victims still experience distinct symptoms of distress. More than a year after the rape, many victims suffer from sexual dysfunction, limited social interaction, suspicion, fears and depression. Because so many of these psychological symptoms are still present in rape victims years after the assault, psychologists believe that many victims never fully recover from rape.

It has been estimated that between 75% and 85% of rape victims who were married at the time of the attack are divorced within two years thereafter.

Using Rape Trauma Syndrome In Court

Historically, rape victims were treated badly by the legal system. Social myths about women as victims of sexual assault resulted in rape laws that made prosecution both difficult and traumatic for the victim. In the 1970s, reform of rape laws shifted the focus of the prosecution onto the defendant's conduct and away from the victim's behavior. While this helped a victim of violent or "stranger" rape, it did little for a victim of date rape because the ultimate issue is usually consent.

Date rape presents a particular challenge for the prosecution for several reasons. First, there are rarely any witnesses to the act, so the victim's own testimony must be used along with whatever circumstantial evidence she can muster. Second, victims of rape, particularly date rape, often do not report the crime immediately. Third, there is often no immediate outpouring of the type of emotion that would be expected following a violent assault. In many cases, there is no immediate display of emotion at all. In fact, it is not uncommon for the victim to return to the scene of the attack or even feel safe in her attacker's presence after the event. This is peculiar to date rape when the parties were previously acquainted. The absence of witnesses, delay in reporting or the absence of traumatic emotion may then lead to the suspicion that the victim consented to the act.

The identifiable physical, behavioral and psychological symptoms associated with rape trauma syndrome can be used in court to explain, among other things, the victims' emotional reaction and why they do not always report the crime immediately. The presence (or absence) of these symptoms has been almost routinely observed in rape victims and can be used as an indication of whether a rape actually occurred. Professionals in rape crisis centers or emergency rooms who are trained to determine whether the victim's physical and psychological condition is consistent with the course of rape trauma syndrome can later testify as to their findings. It is becoming more and more common for rape prosecutors to offer expert testimony of rape trauma syndrome in order to obtain a rape conviction. This is proving to be an increasingly successful strategy.

Must A Victim Resist?

Because of the nature of date rape (an initially consensual social relationship that goes too far and involves unwanted and coercive sexual activity), the question of fabrication often arises. Sometimes this boils down to whether or not the victim resisted her involvement in the sexual activity in order to express her lack of consent. Although there has been no evidence to suggest that victims of date rape are inclined to make false charges, courts have traditionally imposed specific requirements for the prosecution of a rape case. Specifically, in addition to the statutory elements of rape (penetration and lack of consent), the prosecution must show that the victim resisted, that she made a prompt complaint and that she was "chaste."

Some judges believe that resistance does not merely require verbal protests, but also that the victim physically struggle with her attacker. Courts do not uniformly require resistance in all cases of rape, but are more likely to do so in cases of date rape. In fact, in many cases of stranger rape, the victim is not required to resist at all, even if her attacker is unarmed. If the victim is in her own home, she also need not try to leave. The reason that some courts have required resistance is that they seem to believe that sometimes women give mixed signals, and that men have been used to ignoring a woman's words. "No" alone, even when said repeatedly, has seldom been regarded as enough. Therefore, the additional resistance requirement is regarded as putting men on notice that sex is unwelcome.

For many years, courts have also assumed that rape victims would complain immediately to the authorities. This was the so-called "hue-and-cry" theory (now discredited) and led to the premise that a delay in reporting a rape suggested that the rape probably did not happen. Although this theory no longer prevails, its remnants remain in the law's "fresh complaint" doctrine (recognized in some jurisdictions) which puts a victim's credibility in doubt if she did not report the crime immediately. Evidence of the course of rape trauma syndrome has been useful in this regard.

A victim's chastity has historically been another factor which some courts have believed was relevant to whether she was likely to have consented to the act. If the victim had a history of sexual activity, her reputation and, therefore her credibility, would be tarnished. Historically the punishment for rape also depended on her chastity: if the victim was chaste (and from a wealthy family), the punishment was severe; if not, there was virtually no punishment. These traditional stereotypes developed into an institutionalized sexism within the legal system. Beliefs die slowly and today, while the rules have shifted, the view that the victim's sexual history is relevant to her charge of date rape still too often prevails. This is particularly true if she had a previous sexual relationship with the same defendant.

Presenting Rape Trauma
Syndrome Evidence In Court

Date rape is clearly one of the most difficult crimes to prosecute. As stated earlier, the absence of witnesses is a big factor. Other important factors include: victims are ambivalent about prosecuting an acquaintance, even one who raped them; victims question their participation (in retrospect) and wonder if they might have done anything else to discourage or prevent the attack; victims feel concern about whether anyone would believe them; and victims often question whether it is worth the effort. These obstacles, however, are relatively easy to overcome with the appropriate medical and psychological support. The more troubling obstacles for a victim of date rape include providing a credible explanation for why she did not report the crime right away, why she cannot remember significant details of the event, or even why she might not have fled from her attacker as soon as she could.

Readers may recall that the complainant's case in the William Kennedy Smith trial was seriously undermined by her inability to recall certain events during the evening of the alleged incident and by her remaining at the Kennedy estate after the incident. In fact, rape trauma syndrome provides both a clear and credible explanation for each of these factors. Yet it is virtually impossible for a jury to understand that these factors are real, except through an understanding of how such a trauma affects a victim. While it does not seem to make sense if an observer applies standard logic to understand how this could be so, the experience of rape victims confirms that it does happen and often, in fact, the way Mr. Smith's accuser reported.

Evidence confirming the presence of rape trauma syndrome can only be presented through an expert witness who is qualified to report on the issue. An expert is not asked to give an opinion on the defendant's guilt or innocence, but to explain the factors which are in their area of expertise (such as whether the symptoms displayed by the victim are consistent with those displayed by known rape victims).

Assuming that the prosecution has a qualified expert, the discretion of the court still determines whether it wants to recognize the credibility of a relatively new or controversial subject. Most courts require that the subject matter of the expert's testimony reach a certain scientific status in order to be considered reliable. In determining reliability many courts make their judgment in terms of whether the evidence is based on a technique that is generally accepted in the scientific community. Many, but not all, courts have concluded that rape trauma syndrome meets this criterion. The fact that rape trauma syndrome qualifies as a medically diagnosable Post-Traumatic Stress

Disorder increases its scientific legitimacy and gives further evidence of its general acceptance in the scientific community.

Jury Considerations

Some courts have also questioned whether evidence of rape trauma syndrome is helpful to the jury. An expert will only be allowed to testify about an issue that is considered beyond the knowledge of the average layperson. If it is already within the common knowledge of most people, it is not considered helpful. Most people seem to agree, however, that the course of rape trauma syndrome is not within the common knowledge of the average person. Finally, experts will not be allowed to testify if their testimony is likely to prejudice unfairly or mislead the jury or confuse the issues. If, for example, the subject matter is so technically difficult in nature that most jurors could not understand or identify with it — even with the expert's explanations — most courts will exclude this testimony on the ground that the jury would be more confused than helped by this testimony in getting to the truth of what happened.

Critics of admitting evidence of rape trauma syndrome are troubled by two factors which they claim will prejudice a lay jury. First, they point out that the word "rape" in "rape trauma syndrome" implies that the victim has, in fact, been raped when actually that determination has not yet been made. A related (and more compelling) argument is that lay jurors are too accepting of the so-called "expert" testimony. Unless the defendant can afford an expert of his own (most defendants do not have the unlimited resources available to the prosecution), the jury might give undue weight to that testimony without being able to hear another point of view and evaluate it critically.

Further, some skeptics believe that the major motivating factor for promoting rape trauma syndrome has been to combat the widely accepted social myths about rape victims "asking for it," being promiscuous or looking for revenge. While they believe that the myths should be exposed for what they are, they do not believe that a medical syndrome needs to be created in order to discredit these myths.

Considering these factors, most courts have nevertheless ruled in favor of admitting expert testimony of rape trauma syndrome, probably because it is easily understood and a jury is, therefore, likely to be able to consider it fairly. As for the possible prejudice of its title, "rape trauma syndrome," the word "rape" is used often throughout the presentation of the prosecution's case, although the use of this word to distinguish a particular type of medical evidence will do little, if anything, to add to the impact that the word "rape" has on its own.

In cases of date rape, the ultimate issue is whether the victim consented to the sexual activity. The greatest value of rape trauma syndrome evidence is to prove lack of consent in such a case. If the presence of rape trauma syndrome is found, it allows a jury to infer that a trauma has occurred and corroborates the victim's testimony on the issue of consent. Obviously, expert testimony that rape trauma syndrome was found cannot identify who committed the act, but can back up the testimony of the victim that a rape had been committed. In fact, in one case, expert testimony of rape trauma syndrome was allowed to rebut an 11-year-old's disclaimer of charges of rape. She initially made the charge and later recanted it. Evidence of rape trauma syndrome was used to prove that it did, in fact, happen.

Courts continue to refine their positions on rape trauma syndrome. One court has allowed psychiatrists or psychologists to testify as expert witnesses, while precluding a social worker from doing so. Another court stated that rape trauma syndrome was not adequately developed as a theory to determine whether a rape had occurred and not sufficiently recognized in the scientific community. As a result, testimony on rape trauma syndrome was not allowed in that court. Still other courts have held that rape trauma syndrome is admissible testimony only when the defendant bases his defense on the ground that the victim consented to the sexual activity.

Finally, still another court has held that an expert cannot testify that the victim suffers from rape trauma syndrome, but can testify that she has symptoms that are consistent with traumatic experiences generally. Thus the use of rape trauma syndrome testimony, while growing in acceptance, must be carefully considered in relation to the prevailing thought of the specific court trying the case. Most psychologists believe that evidence of rape trauma syndrome is a significant step forward in that it yields a more informed and persuasive presentation of the facts.

LISA'S STORY

I have to begin by telling you that when this was going on, all the time I had no idea that what we were doing was not right. I certainly had no idea that it was illegal. During the three years that Ted and I were having sex and I thought we were in love, my only concerns were that Ted would keep loving me and that my parents would not find out what was going on. There was actually little likelihood that my parents would find out, or even care, because at the time they were going through a divorce and were so involved with being crazy at each other that they had little time or energy for me. As for Ted, he was a master at keeping me on a string using deceit and manipulation.

It all began during the winter of my freshman year in high school. I was just 15 years old. I had been having my period for about three years and thinking about boys for even longer than that. I did well at school and planned on going to college. I enjoyed reading and dreamed of being a writer. My home life was terrible because my parents were always fighting, and I would spend as much time as I could out with my friends. We lived near the ocean, and often a group of us would hang out at the sea wall. One night I went out to get away from a particularly ferocious argument between my parents. I was kind of down and looking for something to distract me from my upsetting thoughts.

While we were hanging out, feeling bored and looking for something to do, a guy came by walking his dog. He was tall and pretty good-looking, even though he seemed a little fat. He looked older — maybe 20 or 21. The dog came over to me and started sniffing around. It was a cute dog and I began to pat him. This was the most exciting thing to happen to me all day. The guy came over and we started to talk about the dog. The guy's name was Ted. He was real friendly and we started to joke around. After a while he said he had to go and asked if I wanted to walk along with him. I was flattered and glad to have something interesting to do. We walked and talked and laughed and had a terrific time.

Ted told me he was 20 and a day student at the local state college. He was an English major and loved poetry, rock music and opera. It was getting late and I had to go home. Ted asked for my name and number and said he would like to see me again. I was thrilled and thought about him all the next day. Two days later he called, and we arranged to meet on the beach.

It was winter, but the cold didn't seem to matter. Ted and I were oblivious to anything but each other. We seemed to get close very quickly and he told me some personal things about himself. For example, he said that he felt very self-conscious about his weight and didn't believe that a girl could be attracted to him. I told him that I thought he was nuts and that he was a very attractive guy. We talked a little more about himself, and before long, he was walking with his arm around me. After a while we went to sit on the sand and began to neck. This was the first "real man" who ever kissed me, and I found myself getting very aroused and very nervous at the same time. He told me how great he felt being with me. He asked me how old I was, and when I told him, he acted very surprised, because he said I was so mature. We didn't do much more that night, but we began seeing each other almost every day. Our relationship seemed to get closer and closer, and within the next couple of weeks we went from petting to real sex, intercourse. Ted went real slow and was very reassuring. He made me feel so good. The sex was terrific. He taught me a lot and introduced me to things that nobody else ever told me about, like oral sex. But what was more important was that he made me feel wanted, important, beautiful and happy. I looked forward to being with him and to even hearing his voice. I found that if a day went by and I didn't hear from him, I became very nervous, preoccupied and depressed. This lasted until he called me.

We continued to have sex as often as we could, mostly at his apartment, and even though I enjoyed it, it wasn't as important as feeling that I belonged to Ted and that he needed and wanted me. As spring came, and we both had to study for tests, we seemed to see each other less and less. The days we didn't get together were very hard, but Ted would always show up eventually and always managed to make me smile. Then he would calm and reassure me that I was special, and we would have sex again.

In early May, Ted announced that he would be going away to work for the summer. I was devastated. He assured me that he loved me and would call me every day. He left without leaving me his phone number. I had to wait for him to call, and he never did. I was beside myself. I couldn't concentrate on anything and only thought about him. I went through every feeling imaginable, from the deepest feelings of love to wanting to kill him. My family was falling apart, but all I cared about was Ted.

One night when I was at my wits end from not having heard from him, I decided to end it all and swallowed a whole bottle of aspirin. I was rushed to the emergency room where my stomach was pumped out. I was alive but very depressed and didn't want to talk to anyone. I was released from the hospital and sent home to be with my very unhappy mother.

Ted never did contact me again. I heard that he transferred schools to finish his senior year. I'm still not over Ted. It's three years later now, and I still get very depressed thinking about him. I also find that I either have little interest in other guys or, if I meet someone interesting, I become so anxious that I scare him away. I'm able to do my school work okay, but I find that I have a lot of physical problems and am never very happy. I don't see my father very much, and I'm not much support for my mother. Mostly, I feel all alone.

What Happened?

Every state has a law or laws about how old a woman has to be in order to consent to sexual relations. If she is below that age, the law says that

she is too young to give "informed consent." Therefore, anyone who has sex with her, either vaginal
or oral, will be guilty of "statutory rape." In addition, most states have laws dictating that if a woman, regardless of how old, is under the influence
of drugs or alcohol and her ability to reason is
diminished, or if she is asleep or diagnosed as mentally incompetent, any vaginal penetration or oral
sexual contact which occurs with her will also constitute statutory rape.

Lisa's situation is a clear case of statutory rape,
since in her state, the minimum age for consensual sex is 16. Lisa was 15 at the time she began
her sexual relations (i.e., sexual intercourse and
oral sex) with Ted. Even though she consented to
the relationship and may have even sought it out
or intiated sex, as a statutory "child," she is not
viewed by the law as being able to give "informed
consent." She is not able to be legally responsible
for making such decisions because she is too
young to be aware of the consequences of her
decision. In short, "consent" of the underage participant is irrelevant no matter how willing she is.
This means that Lisa's consent would not help
Ted in his defense. Furthermore, Ted knew she
was only 15 years old — he knew she was underage, or at least knew she was very young. Despite
this knowledge, however, he seduced and manipulated her to satisfy his own needs, disregarding
the effects that his actions might have on an im-
mature and inexperienced girl who was emotionally vulnerable.

Another feature of statutory rape laws is that
even if the perpetrator did not know how young
his victim was, because she lied about her age or
she looked older than she was, this will not help in
any defense of a charge of statutory rape. The

whole purpose behind statutory rape laws is to protect children against the very sort of harm to which Lisa was subjected. States take the issue of the protection of children within their boundaries very seriously, and statutory rape laws are one example of just how seriously states view this issue.

Predictably, in Lisa's case, the consequences were dire, causing her great suffering and probably long-term emotional and social dysfunction. Like most rapists of this type, Ted will probably go unpunished since the victim's shame, guilt and fear of embarrassment prevent her from seeking help for herself and retribution for her abuse. If Ted is true to form, he will probably, at some point, seduce another inappropriate sex partner. However, with increased public awareness about these crimes, his next victim may be more inclined to expose him and put a stop to his illegal and abusive behavior.

CHAPTER · FOUR

Protecting The Victim In Court: Rape Shield Laws And Related Legal Issues

We repeat: rape is defined as nonconsensual sex. State laws dealing with rape may differ in their wording and even in their coverage, but the element of "nonconsensual sex" is at the heart of all of them. Another term that some states have adopted in referring to "rape" is "sexual battery." This was the term used in the William Kennedy Smith rape trial, as Florida is one state that has adopted the term. Technically the two terms mean virtually the same thing, but sexual battery is probably more descriptive of the true nature of the crime involved because rape is first and foremost a crime of violence, not sex. *Battery*, as lawyers use the term, means any form of touching which the victim finds offensive and to which she

69

does not consent. With sexual battery, that violence is expressed sexually. Obviously, simple battery involves more that a mere tap on the shoulder, but it does not require severe physical injury. The "unlawful application of force" is enough. The concept of "battery" exists both in civil law as a "cause of action" (a legally recognized reason to sue someone) and in criminal law as a crime. Rape, however, is strictly a crime. There is no such thing in the law as "civil" or noncriminal "rape."

An important distinction between a "crime" and a "civil wrong" is that crimes are prosecuted by the state and not by the "alleged" victims of those crimes. The civil law is designed to allow the victim to seek monetary damages for the suffering incurred. In criminal law, it is always the "State," either an individual state government or the federal government, which becomes the "injured party" even though the victim was the party that was actually and personally injured. In fact, the victim becomes merely the "complaining witness" whose main purpose, as far as the prosecution is concerned, is to present evidence in the State's case against the person accused of the crime.

When the William Kennedy Smith case came to trial, the name of the case was "State (of Florida) v. Smith," not "Bowman v. Smith." Patricia Bowman was merely the State's chief witness in its case against William Kennedy Smith.

Another important distinction between a crime and a civil wrong is that in order to bring a successful case, the State must present evidence to a jury which proves "beyond a reasonable doubt" that the accused committed the crime. However, in order to win in a civil suit, the person bringing the suit (the "plaintiff") must only prove to a jury that her version of the facts was more likely what actually happened, based on the evidence she presents in court. (The law refers to this as the "preponderance of the evidence" standard.) "Proving" something in court (or disproving it) depends on who presents the "best" or most convincing evidence. The side that does the best, at least enough to convince the jury according to either of the two standards previously stated ("beyond a reasonable doubt" or "preponderance of the evidence") wins. The problem is that it isn't all that simple in the "real world" as the law sees it.

"Evidence" (or the "facts") as to whether "he" did (or did not) do something wrong to "her" is controlled by a body of law referred to as the "Rules of Evidence." Anytime a case, either civil or criminal, gets into court, the Rules of Evidence come into play. They are extremely technical, but what readers of this book need to know here is that they control which side can get a particular piece of information into court for a jury to hear (or see) and for what purpose this piece of information can be used. No matter what sort of case is involved, either criminal or civil, both sides at trial are trying to do the same thing: get in the evidence which most helps them in their case while, at the same time, trying to stop the other side from getting in the evidence which most helps their case.

But why go into all this about "evidence"? Rules of Evidence control who can say what about a particular matter and why. Rape shield laws are actually part of the Rules of Evidence. All federal courts go by one set of rules: the "Federal Rules," and each state goes by its own "Rules of Evidence." As a practical matter, most but not all states have more or less patterned their rules on the Federal Rules. One must, however, be familiar with the Rules of Evidence of the state in which the trial will take place. States can establish whatever rules they choose as long as no constitutional rights are violated.

Criminal Prosecution And Civil Remedies

In a criminal prosecution, the decision to prosecute a reported rape is ultimately up to a district attorney who must evaluate the evidence against the accused and determine the probability of obtaining a conviction. Regardless of whether the case is prosecuted, however, a victim can always "sue," bringing a civil lawsuit, and attempt to recover money damages as a consequence of the assault. Potential money damages include not only medical expenses and loss of earnings as a result of the rape, but also the dollar value of the pain and suffering associated with it. A civil lawsuit is completely distinct and separate from any criminal prosecution.

As a practical matter, a civil lawsuit will usually follow after a criminal prosecution. This occurs for two reasons. First, criminal matters simply move along faster than civil matters. Whereas a criminal defendant is entitled by law to a "just and speedy" resolution of his case, a civil litigant has no such "entitlement" and can wait years for the case to get to trial. Second, since the criminal standard for a conviction ("beyond a reasonable doubt") is much stricter than the civil standard ("preponderance of the evidence" or "more probable than not"), many victims elect to wait for a criminal conviction so that the lesser civil standard is automatically satisfied and the civil case is a lot easier to present.

Even if the State elects not to prosecute the case as a criminal matter (or even if it does and the defendant is found "not guilty"), a victim can still pursue her civil lawsuit. It is now a more difficult task, however since the district attorney has not proven the most difficult part of the case, "liability," — guilt "beyond a reasonable doubt." Even if the district attorney decides to prosecute and loses, the victim can still sue because of the difference in the criminal and civil standard of liability: The prosecution may not have proven its case "beyond a reasonable doubt," but the victim can still try to prove her case by a "preponderance of the evidence." In both instances, however, the victim will be faced with the negative inference that the prosecution could not prove its case. In some but not all cases this is a difficult obstacle to overcome.

Before Rape Shield Laws

Prior to the enactment of today's rape shield laws, there were no special rules recognizing the unique character of rape. The crime of rape was treated like any other crime. The most general rule on what could be presented in court said that any piece of evidence that was relevant could be let in ("admitted") and anything that was not relevant could not. A "relevant" piece of evidence was any evidence that related to proving that the event or incident in question happened (or did not happen). However (there is always a "however" in the law), a second rule said that even though a particular piece of evidence might be relevant, the judge could still rule to keep this evidence out, if he or she felt that this evidence might unduly influence the jury to make a decision based on its emotions rather than the strength of the facts.

Women who brought a charge of rape had good reason to fear both these rules because great latitude was granted in what was relevant in disputing that charge, whereas what was viewed as too prejudicial to be included was often very limited. This is often still true because of how the crime of rape is defined. Rape is:

1. Sexual penetration of the victim

2. Without consent

To prove rape, both of these "elements" must be proven "beyond a reasonable doubt."

In defending against a charge of rape, the accused may present evidence that he either:

1. Did not have sex with the alleged victim

2. There was consent

In short, what rape defendants would try to convince the jury of was either that: "Hey, it wasn't me who had sex with her" or "Sure, I had sex with her, but she wanted it."

While the prosecution must prove its case "beyond a reasonable doubt," the defense's only job is to present enough facts to plant *any* serious doubt as to either of these two elements in the minds of the jury. Relevant evidence which the defense would try to get in almost always included the "alleged" victim's prior sexual history. To put it bluntly, her previous sex life — with anyone — was fair game. Such evidence was seldom excluded by the judge as being relevant but too prejudicial for the jury. The reasoning behind such rulings ran along two lines: (1) Women who had a sexual history (outside of marriage) were "bad," "bad" women lied, and therefore, women who previously had sex outside of marriage would (or did) lie about being raped; and/or (2) women who previously had sex outside of marriage willingly with others could be expected to have "consented" to having sex willingly with the accused. At the very least, even if the alleged victim really didn't consent to sex with the accused on the occasion in question, his assumption that she was willing to have sex with him, given the alleged victim's prior willingness with others, was perfectly reasonable. The law refers to this latter line of reasoning as the "consent by conduct" or "implied consent" argument. Also included in the "consent by conduct" reasoning is the way a woman dresses, where she goes and with whom she associates. ("What did she expect when she went back with him to his apartment/home/hotel room?") A good everyday way of saying "consent by conduct" is "she was asking for it."

So few limits were actually placed on the type of evidence that the defense could use to counteract the "lack of consent" element in rape, as well as the credibility in general of the alleged victim, that lawmakers, under pressure from both law-and-order and feminist groups, finally felt it necessary to enact special rules limiting the type of evidence that could be used against individuals who dared bring a charge of rape and bring the accused to trial.

These special evidentiary rules are referred to collectively as "Rape Shield Laws."

Rape Shield Laws — What Can They Do?

Rape shield laws are special "laws" or "rules" limiting the evidence about the complaining victim that the accused can present to the jury, and in what way he can use this evidence. The federal rape shield law, Rule 412, was added to the Federal Rules of Evidence in 1978. Various early state versions were also enacted about that time. Several states have even updated their rape shield laws since then. Rule 412 states that the accused cannot get on the stand or put anyone else on the stand to give any testimony evidence about the alleged victim's past sexual history or give any evidence as to what he thought or heard about the alleged victim's reputation in the community regarding that sexual history. He cannot use this testimony to show that the alleged victim consented to sex with the accused. Neither can the alleged victim be put on the stand and be forced to give any testimony about her prior sex life.

During the William Kennedy Smith trial, Florida's rape shield statute, which is similar to the federal rule, was largely what prevented the defense from getting in the fact that Patricia Bowman had borne a child out of wedlock. Other facts about Patricia Bowman's supposed lifestyle were barred for similar reasons. What she may or may not have done willingly with other men and how often is something that neither she nor anyone else could be forced to testify about. Prior to the enactment of rape shield statutes, all of this could be — and often was — fair game. Rape shield statutes have largely done away with the myth that "bad" girls are always willing to have sex, so of course this bad girl consented here, too, type of reasoning. In short, rape shield laws eliminate some of the nightmare aspects of a rape trial for the alleged victim: that of having all her prior sex life and any prior "indiscretions" aired in public for the sole purpose of making her look bad and/or look like the sort of person who would "cry rape" to cover up alleged indiscretions. This is the first part of the federal statute and most of the state statutes.

Is The Victim's Past Behavior Relevant?

The second part of the federal statute dictates what evidence can still be let in to be used in the defense's case. The defense can still introduce evidence about the alleged victim's sexual behavior "with persons other than the accused" to show that someone other than the accused was the source of semen or injury to the alleged victim. This is the "It wasn't me, it was some other guy" defense. Federal and most state rape shield laws will, however, still allow testimony on the prior relationship, if any, between the alleged victim and the accused "upon the issue of whether the alleged victim consented to the sexual behavior." What this "exception" to the rule on the alleged victim's conduct says is that if there was a prior relationship between the alleged victim and the accused, it can still be used to show that it is more likely than not that the alleged victim consented to sex with him on this occasion.

Both of these exceptions to the rule about allowing testimony on the alleged victim's past sexual behavior may still be bad news for women who claim they were raped. Many would argue that only direct evidence of consent, that is consent directly and explicitly given, should be available for the accused to use in his defense to the charge. To date, however, neither the federal rape shield statute nor any of the state statutes are that restrictive. Most rape shield statutes, including the federal statute, do offer some procedural protection. So if the defense wishes to offer evidence against the alleged victim on either of these two exceptions (the accused is not the source of semen or the accused and his accuser had a prior relationship), there are certain things that the defense must do before the judge will allow the evidence to be heard by the jury. Most statutes require that the defense notify the court and the prosecution of its intent to use such evidence before the scheduled date of the trial. Typically, the statutes require that the defense do this "not less than ten days before trial." If the defense fails to do this, the judge must bar the defense from using this evidence. Next, assuming that the defense has notified everyone it is supposed to notify, it must then turn over to the court (i.e., the judge) all of the evidence that it wants to introduce and the judge must then hold a closed hearing with both sides present. The defense must then convince the judge that this evidence is relevant and necessary to its case.

What Rape Shield Laws Do Not Do

"Unchastity" of the woman is no longer considered relevant on the issue of consent under the federal rules and by most states. However, rape shield laws only limit admission of evidence when it concerns the alleged victim's prior sexual history with others, and then only if such evidence has nothing to do with the "source of semen" or "other injuries" suffered by her. Prior sexual history between the alleged victim and the accused is still fair game because practically all courts feel that such evidence must remain available to the defendant if he is to have a chance of a "full and fair defense" on the issue of consent.

Earlier in this chapter we stated that rape is a unique crime. Its uniqueness comes from this issue of consent. It is the only violent crime that becomes "noncriminal" if the victim "consented" to the act — sexual intercourse. Therefore, unlike practically all other crimes where only the state of mind of the accused is at issue, in rape the state of mind of the victim is also an issue.

Since no one consents to be murdered or robbed, the law never considers consent an issue, and consent or lack thereof on the part of the victim is not an element of the crime. The defendant can talk a friend into playing "Russian Roulette," that is, the victim has consented to play, but if he subsequently blows his brains out, the person who talked him into playing will still be held guilty of homicide. Presumably, however, victims of rape can consent to being raped if they allowed themselves to be talked into a situation which ultimately led to having sex with the person who talked them into that situation. If a sufficient indication of "consent" can be shown, then there was no rape as far as the law is concerned.

Rape is the only crime where the victim is asked: How were you acting, how were you dressed, where were you when the alleged rape occurred and why were you there? Rape shield laws will not protect her against such questions; the court may still consider the answers to these questions relevant. The problem for victims of date rape is that the very fact that they went out with the accused can and will be taken as admissible evidence on the issue of consent.

Regardless of whether William Kennedy Smith actually did commit rape, the fact that Patricia Bowman *willingly* agreed to give him a lift back to his family home and subsequently agreed to walk on the beach with him were considered important facts in the issue of consent. These facts, coupled with a lack of strong physical evidence that she tried to fight off the alleged attack, were ultimately fatal to the prosecution's case, at least as far as the jury saw it.

Similarly, the defense in the Mike Tyson trial tried to make much of the fact that his victim *willingly* accompanied him back to his hotel room. Even in cases where the victim can display contusions, lacerations and torn clothing, the charge of rape can be reduced to a charge of simple battery because the prosecution failed to present sufficient evidence (remember, the standard is "beyond a reasonable doubt") that the victim had not consented to the sexual act itself.

With date rape, the victim is also questioned if she communicated her lack of consent hard enough or clearly enough to her alleged attacker. Earlier in this chapter, we brought in the issue of "implied consent" or "consent by conduct." More than mere words can convey a message and words alone may not be enough. Despite enactment of rape shield statutes, the alleged victim of date rape will still be forced to ask herself over and over again whether she did anything wrong immediately prior to the rape. She may then still be required to defend her behavior in open court.

Rape victims can still be required to testify about their behavior with others as observed by their alleged attacker. If the accused can state that, based on his observation of his accuser with others in public (e.g., "sexually seductive behavior"), he thought that the woman would be willing to have sex with him, and he can convince a jury that his belief was "reasonable," then he has a good chance of avoiding conviction based on what is called "mistake of fact" defense.

What this means is that if the defendant can present sufficient evidence about the alleged victim's behavior that led him to believe that the alleged victim was actually consenting to sex based on his observations of that behavior, and the jury can find that this belief was reasonable, than the law will say that he lacked the "requisite state of mind" for rape. That is, he didn't intend to force the woman to have sex against her will, but he thought that she really wanted it. This forces the alleged victim of date rape to present evidence that she did not give consent and/or that the defendant's belief that she did was unreasonable. The burden of proof is heavier on the alleged victim's side. Remember, the complaining victim in a criminal case stands as the accuser in the State's case against the defendant, and the State's burden of proof is the "beyond a reasonable doubt" standard already mentioned.

As a practical matter for victims of rape, the best and most convincing evidence for lack of consent consists of personal injuries, and she must show that these personal injuries were the result of being forced to have sex with the defendant against her will. Threats of injury may not be enough to convince a jury because there may not be any other physical evidence on this issue. Like so many things in the law, it depends on the jury, on the nature of other evidence or on the cirumstances surrounding the alleged rape.

Rape Shield Laws: Looking Ahead

It is still a popular misconception that most rapes are committed by strangers. The rapist jumps out of the bushes or breaks into a house and pounces on his unsuspecting victim. Statistically, however, most rapes are committed by individuals known by the victim. Only recently have the courts and the public together been forced to deal with the concept of date rape. Rape statutes were never written to require that the forced sexual intercourse be with a stranger in order for the act to be criminal. This perception has persisted, however, not only in the minds of most people, but also in the way that the courts apply and enforce the law. Date rape has forced those responsible for the law's enforcement to look at the exact wording that defines the crime.

There seems no way to define the crime of rape without the element of "lack of consent." Whether or not there was consent to have sex will always be the issue. Where many feel the system has gone wrong is in the question of who, in our present judicial system, has the burden of proving — or disproving — consent. Many feel that too great a burden is placed on the alleged victim to prove that she did *not* consent rather than on the defense to prove that the alleged victim *did* consent.

Mistake Of Fact

Another area of the law that has been criticized is in the court's allowance of the "mistake of fact" defense on the issue of consent. Some feel that this defense should be eliminated as altogether irrelevant. Critics point out that by allowing "mistake of fact" as a defense, the law permits the alleged victim's prior sexual history in through the back door. Only evidence directly related to her behavior toward the defendant and only this behavior on the specific occasion when the victim is claiming rape should be considered relevant. This problem is particularly acute when the accused rapist is the alleged victim's date. Just because the alleged victim and her accused were friendly in the past and/or just because she may willingly have had sex with him in the past should have absolutely no bearing on what has happened to bring everyone into court now. Consent willingly given once does not and should not mean that consent can never be withdrawn in the future. At the same time, just because a woman went out on a date does not and should not be taken as a license on the man's part to do anything or be anything other than a pleasant social companion.

Several of the more enlightened countries in Europe have highlighted this problem. In the Netherlands the government has run a television public service spot which says: "If a woman invites you up to her place for a drink, there is a substantial likelihood that having a drink with you is all she wants." Put another way, if a man is not absolutely sure that his date wants anything more, then *he* should assume that she wants something less than sex. If he does want something more, the burden should be on him to find out for sure. He might, for example, simply ask. It should be his responsibility to determine for certain whether or not she is interested in sex. It is *not* her burden to communicate to a certainty that she is *not* interested in sex. In this country, however, this is still not the case.

"If a woman goes into the lion's den, she should expect to be bitten."

Rape And Sexually Transmitted Diseases

As most readers know, one possible consequence of rape is that a victim can become infected with any of several sexually transmitted diseases including AIDS (Acquired Immune Deficiency Syndrome). Assuming that both penetration and ejaculation* occur, either party, but far more often the woman, can contract AIDS or any of the other sexually transmitted diseases (STDs), such as genital herpes or gonorrhea. It is estimated that there is approximately a 5% risk that any completed act of intercourse with an HIV-infected man will result in transmission of the HIV virus (Human Immunodeficiency Virus, the organism that causes AIDS).

Transmission Of STDs

Many states have statutes that make it a criminal offense for a person who has a contagious disease, such as any of the STDs, to knowingly engage in any conduct which has a reasonable likelihood of resulting in transmission or exposure of the disease to another person. The statutes impose criminal penalties and a growing number of states are also permitting civil actions. Criminal penalties specifically include prison terms for violation of their statutes.

Even states that do not specifically recognize transmission of AIDS or other STDs as a criminal offense may still prosecute an HIV-infected person for transmitting the disease to another person. All states have criminal statutes that cover assault, aggravated assault (for serious

---

*It is reported that in a majority of rape situations, vaginal ejaculation does not occur, either due to premature ejaculation or because the particulars of the situation (stress, resistance) prevent it.

bodily injury to another) or reckless endangerment statutes (for reckless behavior that puts another at risk for
serious injury). Such charges have been brought against
HIV-infected persons who, knowing that they are infected
with a virus and can transmit it to another, engage in
conduct or activity that is likely to risk such transmission.

It is not necessary that the victim die or suffer the
serious consequences of AIDS before charges can be
brought. It is necessary, however, that the disease be actually transmitted. The fact that the activity *could* have
resulted in the disease is not sufficient.

Finally, it is also important to note that even if the
individual did consent to the sexual activity that led to
infection, the assault statutes still apply if the victim did
not know that her partner was infected. Only full disclosure of HIV status before intercourse will relieve an infected individual of liability for transmitting the disease.

Rape requires that sexual intercourse or other sexual
activity occur by means of force or intimidation. Some
states distinguish between "rape" and "aggravated rape"
on the basis of whether the woman was injured by the
rapist. If a woman is infected with the HIV virus as a
consequence of being raped, this would constitute an injury resulting in a charge of aggravated rape.

Among the most significant issues that confront a rape
victim is the concern about HIV. Many states do not require mandatory testing for assailants of rape victims.
Thus a victim of rape must wait the period of time necessary to determine medically whether she is a carrier of
the HIV virus and at risk for developing AIDS. Of course,
even in those states, such as Florida, where rape victims
can demand HIV testing of their attackers, there is still
substantial uncertainty about whether the victim was infected if the rapist is found to be HIV-positive. However,
she can be substantially relieved if he tests negative and
this will doubtlessly be a significant issue in her recovery
from the trauma of the assault.

MARTHA'S STORY

Bill and I met at the VFW club when I was 23 and he was 25 years old. We both thought we were ready for marriage, and it was not a hard decision for either of us. Bill seemed like a fun guy. Everyone at the VFW seemed to know and like him. He was pretty easygoing most of the time but when he had a few beers in him, he often got loud and a little too aggressive.

It was good having a place like the VFW to go to and to have friends to enjoy. We would go there two or three times a week. It was pretty expensive to go out that often, but Bill had a good job at the gas company, and I made pretty good money working at the town hall. Our relationship was good, and we had a lot of fun.

Soon after we met, Bill and I began to have sex. He seemed to enjoy himself a lot and always

wanted more. For me, it was okay, although I
never really felt satisfied. It made me feel good
to please Bill, though, and that seemed more important to me than the sex itself. Somehow I
always thought that it would get better once we
were married. I don't know why I thought that,
but I did think that Bill would be more sensitive
to my needs.

We went to Florida on our honeymoon. Bill was
out every night and usually fell asleep when he
got back to our room. Again I figured things
would change when we got back home and had a
normal day-to-day life. You might call me a dream-
er or something, but I guess I just wanted to be
married, and I wanted it to go well.

When we got home, Bill and I went back to
work. At night, Bill would go to the VFW to drink
with his buddies. I would usually stay home and
do chores like the laundry, house cleaning and bill
paying, then flop into bed tired, thinking about my
next day at work. Bill would come home late, usually around midnight, and he was usually pretty
buzzed, if not actually drunk.

This was the time he wanted sex. He would pour
himself a nightcap and come into the bedroom and
begin to move his hands over my body and rub
himself up against me. It didn't matter if I were
asleep. Sometimes he would force himself on me
even if I were asleep. Sometimes, particularly if he
was drunk, he would shake me until I woke up and
insist that I fondle him or perform oral sex on him.
He often cursed or called me names when he was
doing this. It was almost as if I were just a warm
body that he needed to satisfy himself. Sometimes
I would pretend to be asleep or roll over. Then he
would physically force me to do what he wanted.
He was so strong that I couldn't resist, even when

I tried. I was also young and stupid, and thought this was just the way it was for everyone. I felt dirty and ashamed and often thought that I just wasn't a loving wife and that something was wrong with me.

After 18 months, I became pregnant and we had Jenny. I left my job to care for her, and she became my whole life. With the loss of my income and the extra expenses of having a baby, money became real tight. Bill continued to go out and drink even more. He always seemed tense and angry. He didn't talk to me very much and we rarely did things together. As the money pressures mounted, Bill began to get more physically abusive when he came home drunk. If I tried to resist sex, he would yell at me, saying that I was his wife and that I belonged to him whenever he wanted me. If I tried to get away from him, he would slap or punch me, call me names and scare me to death. It always ended with him forcing me to satisfy him sexually. Things would usually get so loud that sometimes the baby would wake up and start screaming. At those times, Bill would get so angry that he threatened to beat the child if I didn't calm her down and give him what he wanted. I always gave in to him.

I was scared for me and the baby and didn't know what else to do. This went on for months. A couple of times things got so bad that the neighbors called the police.

When they came and found out that Bill and I were married, they said it was not their job to interfere between a husband and wife. At one point, I got an officer alone and showed him my bruises and told him that Bill was forcing himself on me. I also told him I was scared Bill would hurt the baby. The officer said that there was nothing he could do in these "domestic disputes." He made Bill take a walk around the block to cool off, but then told me that there was nothing anyone would do as long as I continued to live with Bill as his wife. He also said that I could never prove that Bill forced me to have sex, and that even if I could prove it, most people would see it as a husband's right to have sex with his wife. He did suggest that I leave Bill. Leave Bill? I was so ashamed and scared.

One night Bill came home completely drunk and began to hit the baby and me. He forced me to have sex with him and then fell asleep. As terrified as I was, I bundled up the baby, took a few possessions and some money I had managed to save, and left the house. What followed was another nightmare. I went to a crisis shelter where I stayed for about a week until I could find a room for me and the baby. I got a temporary order of support, but Bill was able to get visitation rights while we waited for the divorce hearing. When Bill would come to visit, he was almost always drunk and usually tried to force himself on me. One night when he was really angry, he hit me, pinned me down and literally raped me. This was the last time. I put up a fight and screamed like hell. The police came and this time they took Bill away because we were separated and I complained of being sexually and physically assaulted. They suggested that I get a restraining order from the court, which I did. This time I intend to follow through with filing rape charges.

What Happened?

Martha was clearly a victim of marital rape. She experienced a typical pattern associated with this type of rape, starting with giving in to her husband's sexual demands reluctantly and ending with his forcing himself on her when his advances were unwelcome and expressly resisted. At this time only Alabama still does not recognize marital rape as a legal offense. Shame and embarrassment about being involved in this type of marital relationship or situation are also common.

It is not unusual for forced sexual activity to continue over a long period of time since coercion, threats and even force are involved, and fear is a powerful tool in shaping behavior. Often a woman must rely on her husband for support. In Martha's case, she was unable to take any meaningful action to stop Bill or get away from him until he threatened the baby. Prior to that, even though the police were called by neighbors who feared for her safety, she could not get anyone with authority to do anything.

Domestic disputes have traditionally been viewed by the police as both a private matter between husband and wife and as a no-win situation in court because the parties are living together. A conviction based on nonconsensual forced sexual activity is almost impossible to obtain under these conditions and not worth pursuing by the police. However, once Martha's maternal protective instincts were mobilized by Bill's threat to harm Jenny and she decided to leave their home, she then created a situation in which Bill could more easily be prosecuted should he rape her again. The additional physical evidence of Bill's assault, including bruises, contusions and torn tissue in Martha's vaginal area, would also contribute to the case against him.

Although she didn't mention it in her story, Martha had received much good support and advice at the crisis shelter and was told to go to a hospital to have her physical condition evaluated, treated and documented. Although Bill never had to stand trial, he was required to stay away from Martha even during visitation with Jenny.

CHAPTER FIVE

The Defendant's Legal Rights In Court

A basic proposition of the criminal law in this country is that anyone accused of a wrong is to be presumed innocent until proven guilty. The burden of proof is on the State, which must prove its case "beyond a reasonable doubt." The situation for the civil (i.e., non-criminal) law is parallel: The burden of proof is on the "plaintiff," the party bringing the civil complaint, and that burden of proof is "by a preponderance of the evidence." The basic focus of this chapter is on the *defendant's* legal rights in court or, more specifically here, the defendant's legal rights in the face of a criminal charge and subsequent trial.

In this country, the ultimate source for the rights of criminal defendants is the United States Constitution.

Generally speaking, these rights are to be found in the so-called "Bill of Rights," which consists of the first 10 amendments to the Constitution. Within the Bill of Rights, the fourth, fifth, sixth and eighth amendments are what concern criminal defendants. The Fourteenth Amendment to the Constitution, which was passed almost 80 years after the Bill of Rights, applies protections contained in the Bill of Rights to all the states. In addition, each state has adopted its own individual constitution which may contain even broader protections than those contained in the federal constitution.

The federal constitution was written at a time when those accused of a crime were at a distinct disadvantage in the face of an all-powerful state, and "guilty until proven innocent" was the rule in practice if not in theory. In this country after the adoption of our Constitution, however, the theory behind the criminal law was that defendants have fundamental rights which need protecting; the "State" which actually prosecuted those accused of a crime did not need specific protection because the balance of power was already on its side. This is still the case today and is why "presumed innocent until proven guilty" is the basic rule behind criminal procedure and the rights this procedure is designed to protect. Those who bring a criminal complaint, the alleged victims, do not figure in this equation because the harm they are alleged to have suffered is seen, in criminal law, as the same thing as harm to the "State." The State is placed in their stead as the prosecuting "party."

The Fourth Amendment

The Fourth Amendment to the federal Constitution and its equivalent state versions protect individuals and their property against unreasonable searches and seizures by the government. Strictly speaking, the rights that this amendment trigger arise before the question of going to court and going to trial arises. The Fourth Amendment provides the most direct protection to criminal "suspects" before there is an issue of whether they actually become "defendants." The Fourth Amendment requires that police have good reason (most often referred to as "probable cause") to believe that a crime has been committed and that the individual or individuals that they seek to arrest were the person or persons who committed the crime. Usually, the police must present sufficient evidence to a judge or magistrate in order to obtain a warrant to search and/or arrest the person they suspect. A warrant is a written order made on behalf of the state which "commands" the police to make the arrest and/or conduct the search desired. Therefore, much of the direct impact of the Fourth Amendment upon the rights of defendants falls outside the scope of this chapter.

The principal area of impact of the Fourth Amendment at trial is on the evidence that the state can present in support of its case against the defendant. As said in the previous chapter, the side that presents the "best" evidence, both up to and at trial, is the side that "wins." The Fourth Amendment has a significant impact on whether or not certain evidence gets to the jury. If the defense can show that certain evidence against the accused which the state would like to present in its case was obtained in violation of the Fourth Amendment ("bad" evidence), it can get this evidence "suppressed," that is, thrown out, before a jury even hears about it, in fact, even before there is a jury. Furthermore, any evidence which is itself all right, but which came as a direct product of "bad" evidence can also be suppressed. Arguments by both sides over disputed evidence occur in front of the judge only, and most frequently these arguments occur during the "pretrial" phase of the proceedings before a jury is even chosen, but after it has been decided that there is enough "good" evidence to bring that particular defendant to trial.

As discussed later, if a person is illegally arrested or detained, the trial court may suppress any statements he makes to the police.

The Fifth Amendment

The Fifth Amendment to the federal Constitution (and its state versions) ensures that the government cannot compel "any person" to incriminate himself or herself, and that the government cannot repeatedly try a person for the same offense. It also provides that the government may not deprive any person of life, liberty or property without due process of law.

1. The Right To Remain Silent

This right is both broader and narrower than one might suppose. Many people do not realize that the right against self-incrimination extends to *any* witness called to testify at any proceeding, not just the defendant in a criminal trial. "Any person" means just that: No one may be compelled to testify against himself or herself. Needless to say, however, witnesses can and will be compelled to give evidence against the defendant in a criminal trial, so long as they are not forced to incriminate themselves. There are also certain "privileges" against testifying against another, such as the "marital confidence" and other "policy-type" privileges. But these can be very complex and are outside the scope of this chapter.

Defendants have an absolute Fifth Amendment right not to testify at all. If they choose not to take the stand, the State cannot compel them to do so. Further, the fact that defendants may choose not to testify may not be considered by the jury as evidence of guilt. Should the defendant choose to remain silent, the judge is required to instruct the jury (usually at the defendant's request) that silence is *not* a sign of guilt.

The Fifth Amendment right to silence is the basis of the landmark case of *Miranda v. Arizona.* The Supreme Court ruled that "the right to have counsel present at the interrogation is indispensable to the protection of the Fifth Amendment privilege." It further held that to protect the right to remain silent, the police questioning a suspect in custody must "read him his rights," a procedure familiar to anyone who has seen police dramas on television. If the police fail to read the suspect his rights, or fail to obtain a voluntary waiver of the right to remain silent and to have an attorney, the prosecution will probably not be able to use the suspect's statements against him at trial.

Miranda applies only where the person being questioned is "in custody" or "detained." A person is "in custody" when he reasonably believes he is not free to leave. It does not apply if the police are merely questioning someone on the street or have only asked the person to come to the station voluntarily to answer questions. Under the Fourth Amendment the police may not take a person into custody (that is, arrest him) without "probable cause" to believe that the person has committed a crime. A police officer also may briefly "detain" someone when the officer can give good reasons for believing that the person may have committed a crime. If the defendant is illegally arrested or detained, the prosecution may be barred from using his statements even if the police comply with *Miranda.* This is because the Fourth Amendment forbids the use of evidence (including statements) resulting from an illegal arrest or detention.

The right to silence protected by the Fifth Amendment is narrower than one might think. It is limited to words and does not generally apply to what might be called "show and tell" or "demonstrative" (nonverbal) evidence and physical evidence. The State can obtain court orders compelling a defendant to give handwriting samples, to speak for the purpose of voice identification, to wear a particular piece of clothing or to display distinguishing marks that may aid in identification.

At a recent rape trial in Maryland, the complainant testified that although she could not be absolutely sure of the defendant's face, she was vividly aware of a very strange birthmark on her attacker's penis. Although the defendant was not required to display his penis for the edification of the jury in open court, he was required to accompany a policeman with a Polaroid camera to another room where a picture of his penis (with the birthmark) was taken for submission to the jury. Such demonstrative testimony was outside the scope of the Fifth Amendment's protection. A conviction was ultimately obtained as a result.

2. Double Jeopardy

The Fifth Amendment protection against repeated trials is called the "Double Jeopardy Clause." In broad terms, it means that the prosecution has only one opportunity to try the defendant for a particular crime. If the jury acquits the defendant, it is all over for the prosecution. "Guilty" means guilty, but "not guilty" can mean either that the jury truly believed the defendant did not commit the crime or that the prosecution failed to present enough evidence to prove his guilt "beyond a reasonable doubt." Having failed to prove its case, the prosecution gets no second chance because the Fifth Amendment forbids it. (If the jury cannot decide on a verdict, the judge will declare a mistrial, and the Fifth Amendment does not prevent a retrial.)

A defendant who has been found guilty can appeal his conviction and may get a new trial if the appellate court feels it is called for. It should be noted here that courts of appeals do not (in fact, cannot) retry the case. They look at the record created during the trial to see if the judge made any incorrect rulings of law that made the trial unfair. If the judges reviewing the record feel that the trial was unfair, they will probably order a new trial for the defendant and the State will have another chance to "do it right."

3. Due Process

In addition to the right to remain silent, defendants have a due process right to be heard in their own defense. The Supreme Court clearly established this right in *Rock v. Arkansas*, a case in which the trial court limited the testimony of a woman charged with killing her abusive husband in self-defense. Thus William Kennedy Smith and Mike Tyson testified at their trials because they chose to, not because the State called them to the stand. Once a defendant takes the stand, however, the prosecution may cross-examine him and attack his testimony. Therefore, the right to testify can backfire against defendants because anything they say can and will be used against them by the prosecution. Furthermore, the right to testify in one's own defense does not include the right to perjure oneself.

Some defense attorneys have been presented with the as-yet-to-be-solved dilemma of what to do when they know their clients were about to lie on the witness stand. The defendant cannot be prevented from testifying if he insists on doing so. On the other hand, the attorney cannot actively assist the client in committing perjury. The defendant takes the stand at his peril, but his right to do so is absolutely protected because the Constitution protects his right to give testimony relevant to his defense, barring a lie.

The Supreme Court has also held that due process requires that the prosecution may not knowingly use false evidence at trial and may not conceal evidence favorable to the defense. For instance, in the leading case of *Brady v. Maryland* the Court ruled that the State had violated due process in obtaining a murder conviction and death sentence while concealing evidence that another person had confessed to the crime. Accordingly, the prosecution must tell the defense if it discovers that any of the prosecution witnesses have not told the truth or that it has found evidence that might help the defense.

Although it is not required by the Constitution, federal law and the law of most states require the prosecution to give the defense at least some information about who its witnesses are and what statements they have made to the police. This information is termed "discovery." Florida is rather unusual in allowing "discovery depositions" of the witnesses prior to trial. At a deposition the witness is put under oath and questioned by the lawyers about the case. The questions and answers are formally recorded and may be used at trial if the witness testimony changes.

A deposition is not a public proceeding. Nevertheless, testimony taken during a deposition becomes a public record to which anyone, including the press, may have access, unless the court orders the records sealed. What comes out at deposition is not necessarily what can or will be testified to at an actual trial. This explains the difference between what the public read in the newspapers about the accusations of three other women against William Kennedy Smith and what the jury at his trial actually heard. It also shows how facts about the victim, Patricia Bowman, got into the press, even though they were excluded at trial (primarily by Florida's Rape Shield Law). Testimony taken during a deposition is not subject to the rules of evidence, but testimony admissible at trial is. Unless the questions are blatantly a "fishing expedition," an attorney can ask anything at a deposition. There is a good news/bad news side for victims. The good news is that unless it is discovered by some means outside of a court record (that is, it is leaked), the name and any other potentially identifying specifics of the alleged victim will not be made public unless she chooses to give her identity.

The Sixth Amendment

Among other things, the Sixth Amendment provides that the criminal defendant has the right to a speedy and public trial by an impartial jury after he has been "informed of the nature and cause of the accusation," and at which time he has the right to the assistance of counsel. Therefore, once a charge has been brought and an arrest made, the state is put under pressure by the Constitution to move as quickly as possible to take all the steps necessary to bring him to trial. This does not mean that an individual arrested today will be brought to trial next week, however. There are several necessary procedural steps in between.

1. Filing The Charges

Before bringing the case to trial, the State must formally present the charges to the court. In a felony case (and rape *is* a serious felony), the document containing the formal charges is an "indictment" or an "information." This document informs the court and defendant of the "nature and cause of the accusation." Before the federal government can bring charges, the Fifth Amendment requires that the charge be made by an indictment entered by a *grand jury*. Although this part of the Fifth Amendment does not apply to the states, many states also require that felony charges be brought by grand jury indictment. (In other states, the prosecution may file the charges in an information.)

A grand jury is a group of private individuals, members of the ordinary public, which meets to hear all the evidence that the State has against a suspect and decides whether there is enough evidence to support the filing of formal charges against him. In short, the grand jury is strictly an investigative body. It does *not* decide guilt or innocence. It decides only whether the quality and amount of evidence is enough to bring the accused to trial. Grand jury proceedings are always closed. If the grand jury does find "probable cause," then it issues the indictment formally charging the suspect with one or more crimes. At no point has the issue of guilt or innocence of the accused been decided. It should also be noted that evidence considered by the grand jury is not necessarily the same as the evidence eventually presented at trial (if there is a trial). A grand jury may hear things in a case which the *trial* jury may not. The grand jury is yet another hurdle which the prosecution may have to jump before presenting its case against the accused at trial.

Once formal charges have been made, the defendant is brought before a judge for "arraignment." The defendant is formally told of the charges and he may plead either guilty or not guilty. If the defendant refuses to speak or enter a plea and "stands mute," the court enters a plea of not guilty on his behalf. An arrest, indictment or arraignment are not to be taken as anything more than they are: The State presented the grand jury enough evidence to justify a finding of "probable cause" that the defendant committed a crime and should be held for trial. Now, and only now, can the issue of a trial arise. This is the public trial to which the defendant (and the public) is entitled.

2. Assistance Of Counsel

The Supreme Court has ruled that the Sixth Amendment right to assistance of an attorney arises when "adversary judicial proceedings" have begun. The general rule (and in the law there are always exceptions) is that this right arises when formal charges are filed and the defendant is brought in for arraignment. Even attorneys and judges confuse this right to counsel with the right to counsel mentioned in *Miranda*, but in a 1991 decision the Supreme Court held that they are actually separate rights.

3. Rights To Confront Witnesses And Evidence

The Sixth Amendment also provides that the defendant has the rights "to be confronted with the witnesses against him" and "to have compulsory process for obtaining witnesses in his favor." Usually the most important witness against the defendant is the victim. The right "to be confronted" carries with it the right to cross-examine. Although the trial court judge has broad powers to limit cross-examination, it must let the defense test the government's case by exposing inconsistencies and prior contrary statements by the witnesses. The Sixth Amendment right of "compulsory process" ensures that the defendant has the right to subpoena witnesses and present their testimony and other evidence supporting his side of the case.

Rights At Trial

At this point, readers may be wondering what has happened to the right to a "speedy" trial given all the mechanics that necessarily precede the actual trial. The answer is that "speedy" is a relative term. Added to the constitutionally required procedure is the fact that all courts, criminal and civil alike, are overburdened and understaffed. Realistically, "speedy" for criminal defendants means "as fast as possible" and "without unnecessary or prejudicial delay." As a practical matter, it may well be months to a year or more before a criminal defendant actually gets his day in court. In civil cases, there is no such right, at least as far as the federal Constitution is concerned, and years may pass before a civil case actually goes to trial. First-come, first-served is the general rule, and cases usually stack up, so long delays in coming to trial are very common.

Finally, there is the right to a public trial. This right can be waived and, in some cases, the parties involved in trials which may involve particularly sensitive issues or individ-

uals, such as children, may request that all or part of a
trial be closed to the public if publicity may impair the
ability of a witness to testify fully or impartially. Over-
whelmingly, however, criminal trials are open to the public
and, while few people actually attend most trials, the press
is often present to give day-to-day newspaper accounts of
any "newsworthy" events that may occur. Blow-by-blow
press accounts of important trials have a long history in
this country. With the advent of television and the appearance of television cameras in the courtroom during
the actual trial, however, the press has become an even
more significant presence during the trial. Few judges
actually welcome the presence of television cameras in
their courtrooms, but increased public awareness and public pressure have made it difficult for judges to withstand
that pressure in most cases.

Clearly, the most extensive coverage of a criminal rape
trial occurred with the case of William Kennedy Smith
when the entire trial was broadcast on international
television. With this trial, much of the country, and perhaps the world, stepped into a courtroom for the first
time. Additionally, the viewing public got an unusual
behind the scenes account of the evidence that was ultimately withheld from the jury, some by virtue of the
rape shield laws.

The inevitable question arises as to whether the purpose of the rape shield laws is undermined when the
public (but not the jury) is given access to the information
which the statutes seek to "shield." Since the underlying
purpose of these laws is to encourage women to come
forward without fear of exposing their prior sexual history, greater publicity would seem to be at odds with
that purpose. Certainly Patricia Bowman gained little
benefit from the rape shield laws, at least as far as public
exposure was concerned. It should be remembered, however, that rape shield laws are part of the rules of evidence, and rules of evidence apply only to what sort of

evidence gets to the jury trial. Rape shield laws do not apply to what sort of information, particularly information that is part of a public record outside of trial, the press may report. Despite increased media coverage, it is the information that reaches the jury and assists it in arriving at a verdict which is of critical importance at trial. It is still true that most trials do not attract a level of publicity that undermines the protections intended by the rape shield process.

The Jury

Traditionally, criminal juries have consisted of 12 individuals plus one backup juror. This is only a traditional rule, however, and the United States Supreme Court has ruled that there is nothing in the federal Constitution which says that criminal trial juries may not have greater or fewer than 12. Most states have 12-member juries, although many states use smaller panels.

The Sixth Amendment provides for trial "by an impartial jury" of the State and district where the crime occurred. Picking jurors is a "big deal." Both the prosecution and the defense get a crack at picking individuals from among those chosen for jury duty. Each side selects jurors who seem to have a point of view most favorable to its side. The legal name for the process of selecting members for a particular jury is called *voir dire*. In practice, the process is not unlike picking players for a professional sports draft. Both sides try to get the best "players" available for their team while, at the same time, trying to prevent the other side from doing the same. It is not uncommon for *voir dire* to take longer than the actual trial. The increased pretrial publicity that is given to the more spectacular "newsworthy" trials has made the process of picking the required number of impartial jurors (i.e., those who maintain the ability to keep an open mind despite that publicity) even more complicated. In addition, both sides now routinely have experts in jury selection to help them spot the best potential jurors.

Judges do have both the power and the responsibility to keep the process from getting out of hand. For example, Judge Mary Lupo, who presided over the William Kennedy Smith trial, informed both the prosecution and the defense that she was definitely going to keep a tight rein on this phase of the trial, and so she did.

The Eighth Amendment

As far as this chapter is concerned, the relevant right that the Eighth Amendment protects is the right against "excessive bail." The concept of "bail" is frequently misunderstood. Bail is not a punishment; it is merely a sum of money that the accused is required to pay the court to ensure that he will appear in court for trial. "Excessive" is a relative term and what is or is not excessive is largely at the discretion of the judge during a hearing specifically for that purpose. The judge decides an appropriate dollar figure based, among other things, upon the seriousness of the offense, the character of the defendant (such as whether or not he has been convicted of a crime before) and his connections, if any, within the community, such as friends or family. Overall, the figure ultimately set is balanced against what the judge deems the "risk of flight." The more serious the crime and the more likely the defendant is to flee, the higher the figure the judge sets for bail.

Frequently, judges release defendants prior to trial "on their own recognizance," which means the judge feels there is little or no risk that the defendant will not show up for trial. If bail is required, defendants who are able to pay it are released from jail pending trial and are "out on bail." Once defendants do show up in court, any sum of money paid for bail is returned. "Jumping bail" means that the defendant, out on bail, has become a "no show" in his own trial. Any money paid for bail is then kept by the court.

A Note About The "Williams" And Similar Rules

Those who watched or read the proceedings during the William Kennedy Smith trial heard much of something referred to as the "Williams Rule." The so-called "Williams Rule" figured prominently during the phase of the trial when the prosecution tried (unsuccessfully) to get additional witnesses to testify about their claimed experiences of Smith's alleged history of sexual aggressiveness with women. In most cases, however, the press failed to explain what this rule was or how it worked. Many people may have been left with the impression that this was some sort of special law that is uniquely protective of the defendant. This is a misconception. The "Williams Rule" is neither uniquely protective of the defendant, nor is the rule unique to the State of Florida. Additionally, the "Williams Rule" can be used by or against either side. The "Williams Rule" is a rule of evidence, or more specifically, a rule of relevance which the disputed evidence must meet before the judge will allow it to be presented to the jury.

The rule got its name in Florida from the case *Williams v. State*. In this rape case, the court stated that evidence relating to similar facts which point to the commission of a crime will be admissible if that evidence was found to be relevant for any purpose except for showing that the defendant was a bad person with a criminal "propensity." There is a similar rule in the federal Rules of Evidence as well as in each of the various state evidentiary rules. They all say virtually the same thing: Just because the defendant has committed or has been accused of committing other crimes, or has a reputation of being a "bad character," these facts will not be admitted in *this* trial for the purpose of showing that he committed the crime of which he is currently being accused. Just because the defendant may be a rotten human being and may have led a "life of crime," these facts are not relevant to whether he committed this particular crime. The general rule is that character evidence may not be admitted to prove conduct on this particular occasion. There are several exceptions, however, and they depend on which side brought the issue of character up in the first place and why they chose to bring it up.

One exception is triggered if the defendant chooses to bring up the issue of character and present evidence about his general reputation for good character (such as calling witnesses who are willing to testify that he is a "good guy who wouldn't hurt a fly"). Once the defendant does this, the prosecution is then free to attack this evidence by attacking the credibility of the defense's witnesses. Conversely, the defendant may offer evidence as to the bad character of his alleged victim, *except* in rape trials. Such reputation or character evidence about alleged victims is barred because of the rape shield laws discussed in the last chapter.

The other major exception which is particularly relevant to "Williams" type rules is that independently relevant *circumstantial* evidence of specific acts may be used by *any party* to establish:

1. motive

2. intent

3. absence of mistake

4. identity

5. the existence of a common scheme or plan.

In the Smith rape trial, the prosecution sought to include testimony by other women who claimed that William Kennedy Smith had raped them under the "common scheme or plan" part of this exception.

"Common scheme or plan" means that the other crimes must appear to be "substantially similar" to the crime for which the defendant is currently being tried. How similar "substantially similar" must be to be admitted is a matter of discretion left to the judge. Some judges appear to be satisfied that the way the other crimes were committed must bear a strong resemblance to the crime at issue before them. Other judges require that the method used to commit these other crimes must bear such a strong similarity to the crime at issue here as to be virtually identical. The defendant has always put on a blond wig before he committed the other rapes, and the attacker wore a blond wig on this occasion; the defendant in the past insisted that the victim put on a mask, and the attacker in this case insisted that the alleged victim here put on a mask.

In the Smith trial, Judge Mary Lupo appeared to have been looking toward the "virtual identity in method of commission ('m.o.')." Since she found no such virtual identity from the evidence the prosecution wanted the jury to hear, she ruled that it should be kept out. This is why the public, but not the jury, got to hear this evidence. Other judges in other courts have been less strict in their standards, and it is quite possible they would have let this evidence in. There is nothing wrong in this. The law allows judges a great deal of discretion in such matters, and higher courts which may get the case on appeal do not like to "second guess" the trial judge unless there was a blatant abuse of judicial discretion at trial.

Whose Rights?

After having read this chapter, readers may understandably come away with the impression that on the issue of the defendant's legal "rights" in court, the deck is definitely stacked against the complaining victim. Readers who do feel this way have a lot of company, much of it from the legal and law enforcement community.

The framers of the federal Constitution came from a world where the system, at least in practice, worked the other way and where substantial injustice occurred regarding the rights of those merely accused of a crime. The

founding fathers felt that all individuals had certain basic
rights ("life, liberty and the pursuit of happiness") which
needed specific protection and they set out to create a
document to ensure this. People accused of a crime ran a
substantial, but necessary, risk of being deprived of these
basic human rights if they were ultimately found guilty of
these crimes. This is why the Constitution was written
the way it was. Before these rights were taken away, it
was absolutely necessary that all available protection was
given to accused individuals before they were actually
deprived of these fundamental rights.

Co-existing with this belief in fundamental, God-given
rights was the belief that government should govern only
with the consent of those governed. Only the "people" collectively could give this consent, and only they could take it
away. This belief affected the structure of criminal law (to
which the "people" consented) in that a crime was viewed
as a wrong done against the social fabric of the community
at large and the laws they consented to, although only one
individual may actually have been physically harmed. Therefore, when a crime occurred, it was for the "people," the
"state," to prosecute, not the private individual. She (or he)
may actually have brought the matter to the attention of
the state, but once having done so, she (or he) became
merely the complaining member of the larger public in that
prosecution. Furthermore, victims already had rights, the
God-given ones; they were not at risk of being deprived of
them by the "state." Defendants also had these same rights,
but unlike the victims, they were in danger of being deprived
of these rights by the state as punishment for their alleged
crime. This provides little comfort for victims of crimes
who have had their lives torn apart because of that crime.

The system as formulated was the reflection of an ideal,
but the system as a working body of law is far from
perfect. There is certainly growing dissatisfaction with
the greater emphasis placed on the need to protect the
rights of criminal defendants as against the relative lack

of emphasis placed on the rights of victims. The system seems to be out of balance, and the advent of the rape shield laws is one example of the feeling that this balance needs to be corrected. More needs to be done, not only with increasing judicial sensitivity to the rights of victims, but also in laws that reflect that increased sensitivity.

DALE'S STORY

During my sophomore year at college, I met a real nice guy named Steve. He was a good student and, although he was not a varsity athlete, he was a terrific intramural player. He was good looking, smart, charming and full of fun. He belonged to one of the most popular fraternities on campus, and I considered myself lucky to be going out with him. Since we were both serious students and involved in other campus activities, we usually saw each other only on weekends. If there was a concert playing, we would go; if not, we might see a movie. We usually seemed to choose public places for our dates. Neither of us was really involved with drinking, although Steve had a reputation of being able to down a few beers with the boys.

We had gone out three or four times, and I always found Steve respectful and fun to be with.

111

After the second date, Steve put his arm around me and asked permission before he kissed me good night. I am basically the studious type and had not dated much in high school. I did, however, know when a boy was attracted to me and certainly knew when he was excited. Steven seemed to be attracted to me, but I did not feel he was particularly excited. Both of us were always very controlled, and it seemed as if we both wanted to take things nice and slow. I wasn't very "experienced" and besides I didn't want anything to interfere with my studies.

During the late fall, the college had a "Homecoming Weekend," a big social weekend which revolves around a special football game. It's designed to bring alumni back onto campus so they can renew their relationship with the college. It's a big party weekend. All the fraternities have major parties with lots of music, food and alcohol. Steve invited me to be his date for the weekend. I couldn't be with him on Friday night since I had a volunteer commitment I couldn't break. I was really looking forward to Saturday night. I had been studying and working hard and needed time to unwind. I was ready to relax and looked forward to being with Steve.

When I got to the fraternity house on Saturday night, the music was blasting. People were dancing and having a good time. It was obvious that the party had started without me, and I felt I had some catching up to do. Steve spotted me when I arrived and rushed over to greet me. He had had a few beers and seemed very happy to see me. He embraced me and gave me a huge hug and kiss. Lots of people were watching, and even though this was how we normally treated each other, it did make me feel special. Steve got us each a beer.

The music was very loud. People were everywhere, and even though it was cold outside, it was very warm in the house. Everyone was drinking, and the beer seemed to go down quickly and easily.

This went on for a long while, and with the dancing and everything, I didn't realize how much I was drinking. Steve kept filling up my glass and kept drinking himself as well. I guess this went on for a couple of hours. Then a slow dance was played, and it was then that I began to feel uncomfortable. During the slow dance, Steve pressed his body against mine and began to move his hands across my buttocks. I could feel his excitement growing, and even though I had drunk too much, I still had my wits about me and began to feel uncomfortable. Steve was starting to do bumps and grinds on the dance floor, and I felt that I had to stop dancing and cool him down.

I told him that I was feeling warm and asked him to go outside for a breath of air. He said it was too cold outside. He then said that he was feeling a little woozy himself and asked me to go upstairs to his room with him so he could lie down for a little while. I was so anxious to leave the dance floor that I agreed, and we went upstairs. That's when the trouble really began. It's funny, I can't remember everything that happened after that. My guard was down a little because of the beer that I had been drinking, but I was far from drunk. Still, there are gaps in my memory of what happened next.

This is what I do recall. Steve made it over to the bed and flopped down. I went over to sit next to him. The music was coming up from downstairs and still sounded loud. Steve reached over and started rubbing my back, and his hand wandered over to my breast. I tried to move his hand away, but he wouldn't budge. He had his arm around me and forced me down on the bed. I told him to stop, but he ignored me. I didn't want to do this. Then he got on top of me, and I couldn't get him off. He was very strong, and all the beer he had drunk didn't seem to weaken him at all. The more I resisted, the angrier and more determined he seemed to become. His face turned red and he called me terrible names. Among other things, he said I was a bitch and a tease, and he would give me what I had coming to me. He was holding me down with one arm while he was tearing at my clothes with his other hand.

I can't remember what happened next, but somehow he got my clothes off. The next thing I do remember was that he was on top of me, and I felt him forcing me to have intercourse. I must have blacked out just about then and the next thing I remember was being very cold. I was outside running in the cold with only my shirt and shoes on. I was sweating and freezing, and my chest ached. I was aware of the pain in my pelvis as I ran. Again, I can't remember what happened next, but I remember being wrapped in a blanket and sitting in the infirmary. I was shaking and felt angry and used. Even though I couldn't remember all the details, I knew what had happened. I felt dirty and ashamed. I didn't think anyone would believe me. I couldn't even remember everything. I had been so stupid. I drank too much, and everyone saw Steve drinking with me and rubbing against me. I went up to his room with him. Nobody forced me to go. Maybe I really was teasing him and leading him on?

This was the worst experience of my life. I never got to finish my sophomore year. I couldn't stay at school. I felt humiliated and guilty. I felt damaged and thought that people were always looking at me with disgust. I had nightmares about that evening and was always tired. I couldn't concentrate on my studies. I lost interest in my extracurricular activities and didn't feel as if I belonged anywhere. I was so depressed that I felt numb and disconnected from everyone. It was horrible.

It's been two years now, and I never did remember everything that happened that night. I'm still haunted by the image of Steve's face as he forced himself on me. Every time the image comes to me, it is as though it is happening all over again.

What Happened?

Dale was a victim of another typical type of date rape. Since this occurred on a college campus, it is also representative of "campus rape." In fact, this is one of the most common types of rape and occurs far more often than the situation in which an unknown person overcomes his victim by surprise, use of a weapon and violence to force sexual relations.

Date rape typically follows a pattern. The perpetrator is known and is generally trusted by the victim. The couple spend a long time together, and alcohol or drugs are often involved. The rape itself usually occurs in either an automobile or in the residence of one of the couple. A weapon is rarely involved and threats of violence are not usually part of the pattern, although other forms of coercion may be used.

The act itself has been described as having three identifiable stages. The first stage involves the rapist making the woman feel uncomfortable by kissing or caressing certain parts of her body in public. If the woman doesn't unequivocally object, the perpetrator moves on to escalate his behavior so the victim asks to leave the embarrassment of being in a public place. Once alone in an isolated area, the third stage occurs as the rapist forces the victim to engage in unwanted sexual activity.

Dale's case is also a good example of Rape Trauma Syndrome. She has difficulty remembering all the details of her rape. No one is quite sure why this occurs, but it is not an uncommon symptom. Additionally, she began to have nightmares about the rape. She could not concentrate on her work, lost interest in those activities she used to enjoy, felt detached from other people and had to leave college and the reminders of the traumatic event. She experienced shock, physical pain, confusion, guilt and embarrassment. These symptoms can be short lived, lasting six months or less in acute cases, or can become chronic as in Dale's case. Two years later, she is still suffering and is still somewhat dysfunctional.

CHAPTER SIX

Campus Rape:
A Separate Issue?

Is campus rape a separate issue? Yes and no.
Certainly, rape is rape no matter where it occurs.
So, in that sense, there is no difference whether rape
happens on campus or whether it occurs elsewhere. We
have already discussed the phenomenon of campus rape
as a species of date or acquaintance rape, but as a different
breed within the species. The underlying question here is
whether the college rapist differs in his psychological profile from the "typical" rapist. Does he have attributes and
characteristics that are unique to that population and setting? Campuses are special places with a social character
all their own. Whether a college campus is located in a
small college town or in an urban setting, whether most

of its student body is housed on or near a campus, and whether the majority of students commute to class, campuses are little self-contained worlds (microcosms) within the larger world.

Facts And Figures

The incidence of rape on campuses across this country is rapidly on the rise. The most recent statistics suggest that at least one in four college women will either be the victim of rape or will have fought off an attempted rape during her four years at college. This figure translates to over 6,000 sexual assaults per year, or 1 every 21 hours. Despite this high number, less than 5% will be reported to authorities and only 40% of this number will result in some sort of disciplinary action against the attacker.

Additionally, the vast majority of all violent crime on campuses is either drug or alcohol related. Moreover, according to testimony before the United States Congress, 85% of the perpetrators of this violent crime are fellow students, and fellow students are responsible for approximately 78% of the sexual assaults that have occurred on campuses. This is a far cry from the hallowed halls of academia so loved by Hollywood or the great intellectual adventure portrayed in high school graduation speeches. It is much closer to a "hot-house" or a pressure cooker.

Most students who live at or near a college campus are away from home for the first time in their lives. Put bluntly, they are away from familiar surroundings as well as the care and control of their parents or guardians. Most students are between the ages of 18 and 22 when they go away to college. As a result, they are particularly vulnerable to the peer pressure and insecurity that are characteristic of young adults. There is just as much pressure to impress the members of one's group in college, especially in the first years, as there was in high school. Furthermore, many, if not most, college students take with them the attitudes toward dating and male/female social dynamics that they had already formed while in high school and earlier.

Rape has occurred on college campuses ever since young men and women have gone on to higher education together in significant numbers. Prior to the 1960s, however, the opportunities for rape, other than the classic "stranger rape," were significantly limited. The legal position of virtually all colleges and universities toward their students was that of *in loco parentis* which means "in the place of the parent." Colleges and universities were regarded by others and by themselves as their students' "parent" away from home. Young men and women were required to live in campus housing if they were not living at home, and housing for the sexes was strictly segregated. It was not uncommon, for example, for all-male and all-female dormitories to be located at opposite ends of a campus from each other. Similar geographical separation was also the norm for fraternity and sorority housing. In addition to segregated living, no student of either sex was allowed for any reason beyond the lobby of the opposite sex's housing. All campus social functions were carefully chaperoned.

The social upheavals of the 1960s had as profound an effect on the *in loco parentis* doctrine as they did on all other aspects of campus life. By the early 1970s the doctrine was virtually dead. It is notable that it was also in the 1970s that most states changed the age of majority from 21 to 18. Along with the end of *in loco parentis*, desegregation of the genders in campus housing became the norm. Only the fraternity and sorority housing remained untouched, at least as far as regular living was concerned.

Young men and women demanded greater (if not total) autonomy in their private lives, and they got it — and then some. Colleges and universities, for their part, backed away from the *in loco parentis* doctrine and, at the same time, refused to be held legally responsible for any "extraordinary occurrences," such as violent crime on campus, especially if both the alleged victim and the alleged perpetrator were students. Students were seen as full adults who could look after themselves. The college no longer stood "in the place of the parent," and, therefore, was no longer responsible. In addition, because colleges and universities no longer saw themselves or were seen by others as being the "parent" away from home, there was little incentive for them to change on-campus security measures regarding the safety of students, the "campus police," beyond what had been in effect in the *in loco paren-tis* days when watchful "dorm mothers" and/or counselors kept an eye on all that went on inside the dormitories, fraternities and sororities.

The end result of this shift was that colleges and universities went from being too involved in the lives of their students to not being involved enough. Colleges now assumed little responsibility for the safety and security of their students, and denied legal responsibility for any harm that occurred to them at the hands of a "third party," not the college or university itself.

In practice, what this meant was that a student had a better chance to obtain redress for injuries suffered as the result of slipping on a wet floor in her dorm than she had in seeking redress for injuries suffered as the result of a physical attack, sexual or otherwise, on the campus grounds. In short, "security" on campus increasingly meant the security of the college's physical plant, its buildings and grounds, rather than the security of its students while on, in or near these buildings and grounds. College campuses became "ideal" arenas for the seemingly explosive increase in violence, the magnitude of which is only now being recognized.

The Psychology Of The Campus Rapist

Studies suggest that male college students do, in general, tend to engage in a wide variety of sexually coercive behaviors, which range from touching or kissing a woman without her consent to forcing her to perform specific sexual acts characteristic of rape. This research on sexual aggression in college males usually relies on anonymous self-reporting with limited opportunity for these men to be carefully studied. Nevertheless, since most college students fall squarely in the age category of "typical" rape offenders, they would differ, if at all, either on the basis of living in a campus environment or because of socioeconomic factors, being in a position to attend a college with a campus.

As for the campus environment itself, it offers a unique set of peer and academic pressures which probably contribute greatly to males sexually assaulting female students. In one study, for example, 53% of college males reported kissing a woman against her wishes, while 15% reported having forced a woman into a sexual act at some time in their lives. In fact, only 39% reported that they had never coerced a woman into any sexual involvement. One factor that was relevant to whether the college male was likely to engage in sexually coercive behavior was his attitude toward women. If he perceived women to be seductive (by making physical contact, teasing or playing hard-to-get), he was likely to try to force a woman into sexual activity.

Another important factor involves the male's attitudes about rules of social order, including personal responsibility for one's behavior. Specifically, males who demonstrate low levels of maturity, responsibility and social conscience are typically those who engage in a wide range of inappropriate behavior, often associated with delinquency and antisocial personalities. They also seem to be angry men who harbor high degrees of hostility toward others. Such males, particularly those with poor socialization, perceive women as adversaries, undeserving of trust or respect. When they encounter a woman, they act out their hostility by treating her with contempt, including using her for sexual gratification.

The reason that coercive sexual behavior has become such a widespread phenomenon among college males is not entirely clear, but it is most likely due to the convergence of several important factors. College presents for many the first experience of living on one's own away from home. Young men are typically not prepared to function without supervision, with a lot of freedom and limited accountability. Also the extensive use of alcohol and drugs on campuses contributes to the reduction of inhibitors, the relaxation of behavioral controls and the impairment of sound judgment. Additionally, the pressure of academic competition can result in lowered frustration tolerance and behavior which is expressed in a semisexual aggressive manner. Another factor is the desire for male bonding (discussed in Chapter 2), as indicated by the popularity of fraternities, which leads young men to perform all kinds of aggressive acts, often on a dare, and usually to prove themselves to each other. A male cultural context in which women are depicted as manipulative and seductive objects of sexual gratification combined with opportunity, immaturity and reduced behavioral control, due to the use of alcohol and drugs, contributes to his willingness and availability to engage in coercive sexual acts.

How, if at all, does this profile differ from the non-campus rapist? The answer is that, other than the fact of his being in college, this rapist is essentially indistinguishable from any other acquaintance or date rapist. Meeting and talking to him offers no clues that he is capable of committing a violent sexual act. The campus rapist is thus not only indistinguishable from other date rapists, but also may not differ from other "normal" males, except to the extent that was discussed in Chapter 2.

Where Is The Law Today?

Responses In The Courts

The increasing occurrence of sexual assaults and other violent crimes on college campuses has brought another shift in the evolving way the courts and the law generally view the legal responsibility of colleges toward their students. Before 1975 attempts to make colleges liable, legally at fault, met with little success. This began to change in the early 1980s.

In 1980 West Point Military Academy was sued in federal court for harm suffered by a member of a female choral group when she was raped by her escort, a West Point cadet, provided to her by the Academy. The woman prevailed. Shortly afterward, state courts in Massachusetts, New York, California and Pennsylvania ruled that colleges could be found legally at fault for harm suffered by their students under certain conditions. Generally, the standard was whether or not the college administration knew or should have known of the likelihood (the law calls this "foreseeability") of serious crime and/or injury to their students from fellow students or from outsiders allowed to roam freely about the residences and other parts of the college grounds without authorization. As one court pointed out, just because colleges were no longer considered responsible for the moral well-being of their students, as they were under *in loco parentis*, this did not mean that these colleges were not responsible for their students' physical safety.

Colleges can now be found civilly liable in the following situations:

- Numerous crimes have already been reported in or near residences, but the administration has failed to respond with adequate security to check on and control access to these residences.

- Colleges have promised to undertake some responsibility for the physical safety of their students and have failed to perform as promised.
- Colleges have been aware that students have been the victims of violent attacks by fellow students and others, yet have failed to provide adequate information, such as warnings to their other students about these attacks.
- Colleges knew or should have known that behavior by some of their students was or was likely to get out of control in certain situations, such as at parties, and cause physical injury, either to fellow students or nonresident visitors.

Thus the message now being sent by the courts to college administrations: If they knew or should have known that unsafe conditions existed because of their inaction or negligence, they can be sued in civil court for the harm their inaction or negligence caused. What this means for the victims of violent crime on campus is that they and/or their families can now go to civil court and sue the college or university for damages, to compensate for their injuries.

Responses By Legislatures

Despite the increased willingness of courts to impose legal responsibility on colleges and universities for failure to secure the safety of their students, a great many people have felt that not enough was being done to deal with this growing problem. It became increasingly clear that although victims of sexual assault and other violent crime on campus now had an easier time seeking redress for their injuries, a better solution would be to force colleges and universities to prevent, whenever possible, such assaults from occurring at all.

Such preventative measures eventually took two forms: Colleges and universities were forced to "beef up" their security and were required to provide complete and accurate reports on the number of serious crimes that had occurred on or near their grounds each year. The occurrence of several particularly savage sexual assaults on college campuses spurred the legislatures of several states to enact laws forcing colleges and universities to provide complete disclosure of crime statistics on their campuses to all current students as well as to all who had submitted an application for admission. Pennsylvania's College and University Security Information Act, one of the first laws of this type, requires that each college and university within that state provide applicants, students and employees with a copy of that institution's security policies and procedures.

These institutions must also provide information on such matters as the number of students enrolled and the number of students living on campus, the administrative office responsible for campus security, the types of security systems used and all campus policies regarding drug and alcohol use and criminal activity. Furthermore, colleges and universities which have student housing are required to provide descriptions of available housing, dormitory security measures and policies regarding visitors and overnight guests.

Any college or university in the state which failed to comply with the provisions of the Act could be fined up to $10,000. Several other states (Illinois, Indiana, Massachusetts, Missouri, New Jersey, New York and Washington) are considering similar legislation.

Not all states have passed such tough legislation because they already have adequate reporting laws on their books. In 1990, however, Congress, citing the severe increase in the incidence of violent campus crime, decided to pass the Student Right-To-Know and Campus Security Act which, as of September 1, 1992, required all colleges and universities receiving federal funds to provide annual statements of policy and crime statistics.

Additionally, there is currently another bill before Congress entitled the "Campus Sexual Assault Victims' Bill of Rights" which was introduced by those members of Congress who felt that insufficient attention has been given either to the severity of campus crime or to the sheer numbers of women who are the victims of sexual assault on campus. This bill in its current form lists ten basic rights, which its drafters feel victims of sexual assault should have. These rights include:

- The right to be free from pressure by college authorities not to report the crime to campus officials or local police.

- The right to counseling, alternative housing and transfer of classes upon the victim's request.

- The right to be free from suggestions by campus authorities that survivors are responsible for their assault, contributorily negligent or assumed the risk of the assault.

The Response On Campus

Regardless of pending legislation and its enforceability, the problem of rape on campus will never be completely eliminated, barring a necessary change in social attitudes of would-be rapists toward violence against women. Many colleges have voluntarily implemented various preventative measures in response to the rising numbers of sexual assaults on campus and the increased likelihood of lawsuits.

Many student-student sexual assaults have been shown to be either alcohol or drug related. To this end a significant number of colleges have taken steps to severely limit both the availability and the amount of alcohol and drugs on campus. Typical measures have included the total ban of alcohol from campus activities and areas, the changing of campus night-time gathering places from virtual drinking clubs to social centers where no alcohol is served. In response to the fraternity party/alcoholic bash tradition (the type of situation of which Dale was a victim), some colleges and universities have either restricted the presence of alcohol at such gatherings, shut them down or allowed them to serve alcohol only after the servers have completed on-campus training programs on alcohol responsibility.

In addition, many states have increased the drinking age from 18 to 21, thus removing the issue of whether alcohol will be available at most campus locations. Additional measures have been to make available to all students information on crime prevention and awareness, and to make sure that all students — of both sexes — are aware that they are potential targets of crime and teach measures in self-protection and general safety tips. Security measures both around and within dormitories have also been strengthened. Some colleges and universities have initiated "crime-watch" programs and encouraged students to participate as lookouts and report any indications of suspicious activity on campus. Still other colleges and universities have provided escort programs to provide security for students to and from libraries and classes after dark.

Increasing numbers of colleges and universities now require that all incoming freshmen attend sexual assault awareness classes in which members of both sexes, but particularly males, are shown not only what sexual assault is, but also what it does to the victims of such assaults. Such classes typically stress the meaning and importance of "No" and how to avoid situations when a dating or acquaintance relationship could get out of control. Several of the larger universities have also opened Sexual Assault Prevention and Awareness centers or workshops. When sexual assault has occurred, college and university infirmaries increasingly provide rape counseling and a supportive environment to the victims of sexual assault, which not only assists in their eventual recovery, but also makes them aware of legal action, both civil and criminal, that they can take. This is in contrast to the traditional university attitude which was to keep the assault quiet, both to protect the university from liability and to reduce the likelihood of adverse publicity.

Attitude Changes

Clearly, sexual assault on campus is a serious problem. The reactions in the courts and by legislators have increased efforts to alleviate this problem, at least to stop the ever-increasing numbers of sexual assaults and other violent crimes on campus. The very detail in reporting both the numbers of violent crimes and the security measures in place required by both federal and state laws shows a genuine attempt to prevent, as much as possible, the incidence of violent crime. Students themselves have also become increasingly aware of their vulnerability to such violence through programs that educate all students about the seriousness of this problem. Much still needs to be done, however, to change basic attitudes about the acceptability of violence toward women.

A recent study of students from the sixth through ninth grades found that one-fourth of the males felt that forced sex was okay if the man had spent money on the woman, and over two-thirds of the same population felt that forced sex was okay if the couple had been dating more than six months. Coincidentally most victims of sexual assault, whether or not the victim is a college student, are young women between the ages of 18 and 24. In short, it is more the environment (which is relatively closed) and the population (which is relatively identifiable) rather than the criminal act which makes campus rape "special." Such "specialness" has triggered special responses in the law not given or generally available to victims of acquaintance/ date rape in general.

ALISSA'S STORY

I was 17 when I was raped but it wasn't until I was 22 that I realized what had happened. I had dated a fair number of guys throughout high school and did my share of kissing and petting, but I never got into anything heavy.

My parents had talked pretty openly with me about sex and really wanted me to wait until I was ready. I respected them and their values and deep down I believed they were right. Anyway a few times I had to deal with a guy coming on too strong but I always managed to get him to stop before things got out of hand.

For the most part I would say that I had a good childhood — caring and responsible parents and a supportive home that probably few kids actually really get. As I look back at it, the rape probably happened because I was too outgoing and too naive, and I never really thought that something bad like that could ever happen to me.

It happened on a date and the whole thing was over so quickly, I never would have imagined that five years later its effects could be so profound. I was at a party with a guy who I really liked and really respected. But I'm still embarrassed to say, I had had too much to drink. We were both drinking and when my date asked me to go outside and sit in his car, I didn't object. In fact, I didn't even really realize what was happening to me when he started to undress me because he was talking so quietly and calmly. Very quickly, though, I got very scared because I remember telling him "No!" several times and he just kept going as though he never even heard me. I know he did, though, because at one point I scratched at him and he pinned my arm under his knee. When it was over, I couldn't even look at him and I left right away.

The next day I was very upset but I wasn't even sure exactly what had happened. I knew I had had sexual intercourse because it hurt so much and I was still sore the next day. What I wasn't sure about was whether I had somehow led him on. It happened so quickly that I barely said anything. I could have screamed for help, but I didn't even think of it. I was so stupid, I never even saw it coming. And I was so ashamed and embarrassed that I couldn't tell anybody what happened. Instead I decided to quit my job, move back home and try to put the whole incident behind me. My mother used to say, "Time heals all wounds," and I needed time. Unfortunately I learned that even mothers don't know everything.

After a few weeks I calmed down, and gradually I started to get my life back together. After a couple of years, things were actually going well: I had moved back out of my parents' home into a nice apartment. I had made new friends and my career was moving along. I never talked about the assault and actually I didn't even think about it. It seemed that I had put that awful night behind me. Then I met Ted.

Ted was from my hometown. He was a few years older than I. He was kind and gentle and he seemed to really care about me. He had no trouble showing his feelings. But for me it seemed that the closer I felt to Ted, the more anxious and even depressed I became. It made no sense. I had mood swings like I had never known before, for no apparent reason. I found myself feeling frightened and suspicious of my co-workers and even my friends. Ted was very patient with me, but he obviously didn't have the foggiest idea what was going on. Some days we would have fun together. Other days it was so upsetting to even have him get close to me. Usually I would let him hold me and maybe hug me, but I always got uptight if it seemed as if it might go any further. Ted would try to talk to me about it, but my eyes would fill up with tears and I couldn't respond. We were both very frustrated and neither of us understood why this was happening to us. All I knew was that I couldn't help it. These thoughts and feelings would just come to me and I knew that I was out of control.

After this went on for a while, Ted started encouraging me to get counseling. He always said he would stick with me if I got some help. I resisted and resisted but finally after feeling horrible for weeks and being scared that I would lose Ted, I agreed to see a counselor.

The counselor knew there were reasons why things were the way they were and was able to help me to talk about what happened that awful

night years before. It was so hard just to think
about it. Here it was three years later and I was
telling someone about it for the very first time.

As I shared my experience with my counselor,
all the ugly feelings and doubts about myself came
back as though it had just happened yesterday.
My counselor was wonderful: accepting, nonjudg-
mental and wise. I began to see that I had, indeed,
been raped on that date and had not brought it on
myself. I saw how I thought I had put it all behind
me by changing jobs and moving away, but in reality nothing had been resolved. More importantly,
I began to see how the difficulties in my relationship with Ted were the result of this trauma.

So here I am five years later and I'm just beginning the process of understanding and resolving
my experience so that I can truly gain control of
my life. It hasn't been easy and I know it will take
some time, but now I see that time can heal if you
let someone help and are determined to see it
through.

CHAPTER SEVEN

The Healing
Process

The experience of being raped is described by victims as a violent and hostile violation in which each victim, regardless of the level of brutality, fears that she is going to be harmed. Whether stranger or acquaintance rape and with a weapon or not, the ultimate terror is of being physically harmed or killed. This experience takes from the victim's psyche any sense that she has control of her life, her physical being or the circumstances in which she finds herself. It is a totally disempowering experience which in a flash destroys any illusion of safety which the victim may have had. When the perpetrator is known to the victim as a date, relative or acquaintance, the effects can be even more devastating. Women learn to avoid rape by avoiding strangers or situations in which they are isolated. Yet when a woman is raped by an acquaintance, she questions her ability to trust herself, her perceptions and her judgment. Date rape is not viewed as a random act of violence in which the victim finds herself in the wrong place at the wrong time. This type of rape is seen by the victim as a very personal act and one to which the typical response is self-blame, profound vulnerability and a sense of loss of control.

The Recovery Begins

A victim's recovery from a trauma such as rape usually begins at a point following the acute phase of rape trauma syndrome. At this point she has probably already sought medical attention if she chooses to do so and has probably already made a preliminary decision as to whether or not to report the crime to an authority. If she has chosen not to, she may ultimately change her mind through her process of recovery. She may also have an idea of whether her case is likely to be prosecuted, making her a witness in a criminal trial. Recovery from rape and the phases of rape trauma syndrome requires the victim to work through a number of issues.

Task 1: Yes, It Was Rape

Carol was raped by Larry in her own apartment. They had been out together for the evening and both had had a couple of drinks. It was their second date and Carol did not object when Larry offered to escort her back to her apartment.

As soon as they entered, Carol sensed that Larry was acting a bit strange — both nervous and agitated. She realized that she was feeling a little light-headed herself and initially ignored Larry's change in temperament. Within a short time Larry made it obvious that he wanted to have sex. At first she thought she could

gently resist without destroying this budding relationship. Larry became more determined and his behavior
more coercive. At this point Carol began to actively
resist but her efforts were of no avail. Larry forced
himself on her and then left almost immediately after
he was finished.

Carol's first reaction was one of disbelief. She
thought that she had made it clear that she didn't want
sex, but Larry kept going. Should she have done something else? What could she have done? When she awoke
the next morning the effects of the alcohol having fully
worn off, she was furious at Larry but also angry at
herself for having allowed this to happen.

Probably the most important strategy for coping with
sexual assault is acknowledging that it happened and putting the responsibility where it belongs. Many victims of
date rape feel that because they knew their assailant, the
attack was less real, less criminal and less traumatic. It is
not. While the effects on the victim may be somewhat
different from those experienced by victims of stranger
rape, they are no less profound and in some cases the
coping strategies may be even more challenging. Moreover,
due to self-blame, shame, guilt and embarrassment, such
victims are less likely to seek help from family, friends and
professionals, thus placing themselves more at risk for the
long-term consequences of being depressed, fearful and
anxious about certain situations and suffering from dis-
turbed social relationships and sexual dysfunction.

Victims of date rape often question whether or not it
actually was rape and whether they somehow "asked for
it" or otherwise contributed to their victimization. Their
consequential guilt or self-blame makes it more difficult
to reach out for help or accept it when offered.

Therefore, the first step in the process of recovery is
not to deny that it was rape and not to assign blame
unless the victim actually did somehow participate. No

woman "deserves" to be raped or otherwise coerced into sexual activity against her wishes and if she is, it is rape, pure and simple. The sooner she comes to terms with the issue of self-blame, the sooner she can begin her recovery.

Victims also often blame themselves for having used poor judgment in allowing themselves to be victimized. Even when they acknowledge that it was clearly an assault, they blame themselves for failing to heed the warning signs, allowing themselves to become intoxicated or making other poor choices that contributed to their victimization. Some of the self-reflection may be justified. Victims often, but certainly not always, do ignore warning and even danger signs. Nevertheless, victims need to understand that ignorance and poor judgment do not in any way excuse or justify an attack; a woman is no less a victim merely because she could have done something differently.

Task 2: Talk, Talk, Talk

> *Peggy* was assaulted and raped by a co-worker who was employed as an assistant manager in her company. She was a sales associate and desperate to keep her job. After the incident she made the decision not to report it, primarily because she knew it would be her word against his and she was afraid that her job would be in jeopardy. With a young child at home, she couldn't take the risk. Peggy also thought that if she told people, particularly at work (where many of her friends were), the word was likely to get out. For weeks she told no one, but the effects of the assault were evident to her. She had repeated nightmares, was afraid to leave her apartment and began to withdraw, even from her closest friends.

After experiencing a trauma, there is no substitute for a victim being able to share that experience with a warm, sympathetic and empathic listener, who will calmly and patiently let her express her pain. The help need not be from a professional mental health worker, but it does require a compassionate and helpful listener, who is willing to make himself or herself available whenever the victim needs to talk. Family and friends are often reluctant to talk about a rape, often in fear of further embarrassing, shaming, causing pain or stirring up memories of the trauma. ·

Family and friends are often reluctant and uncomfortable simply discussing the subject of rape. They may have their own questions, wondering how the victim might have contributed to her attack and what she might have done to prevent it. Moreover, many well-wishers avoid discussions with the victim or even being with the victim because they do not know how to deal with distressed, tearful, angry, anxious or depressed reactions.

Unfortunately, even among those who are willing to listen to her pain, many offer well-intentioned advice which the victim is either not ready for or which is ill-advised. At the same time victims may also be reluctant to talk to trusted family and friends because they feel that their victimization resulted from the betrayal of a trusted relationship; they are skeptical about reaching out to another trusted relationship.

The therapeutic value of talking about a traumatic event, such as rape, is gained primarily from the victim's ability to understand and validate her own feelings and experiences. Ambivalence and self-doubt can be worked through and the reality of the experience acknowledged and validated. What the experience means to the victim can be processed. Ultimately finding that meaning will assist her in putting the event into perspective and integrating it into her life.

At this point it is important to note that while many of the tasks to recovery are useful and recommended by professionals, the choice to proceed should always be given to the victim. Since the victim experienced a profound sense of loss of control, it is crucial to her recovery that she be given the opportunity to decide what she is going to do, what she is going to allow to be done for her and when things will take place. Well-meaning individuals trying to be helpful may inadvertently undermine the recovery process by feeling that the victim is too upset to make decisions for herself and thus making them for her, leaving her feeling further disempowered.

Task 3: Addressing The Practical Concerns

Jan was raped by Tom, whom she had dated for several months but ultimately had broken off the relationship when she met and started dating Jack. Tom showed up at her apartment one night just a few minutes after Jack had left. Almost immediately after she let him in, Tom sexually assaulted Jan, leaving her bruised and angry. Afraid that Jack would be suspicious of why Tom was at her apartment, Jan decided not to report the crime. She did tell a few of her girlfriends but she refused medical care. For months she struggled with the dilemma of not letting Tom get away with this violent act but not wanting to report it and risk having Jack find out. She also knew (or rationalized) that the process of prosecuting a rapist, particularly an acquaintance, was as upsetting as being raped and didn't want to go through it again.

Getting Medical Attention

A woman who is physically harmed as a result of her assault is likely to present herself first at a medical facility or be brought there immediately by the first person to assist her. More often, however, she is not physically harmed and thus may not seek medical attention. This is a mistake. Victims should obtain medical care for a number of reasons, not the least of which is that it helps her validate the experience in her own mind and minimize the likelihood of later self-doubts and denial. In addition, the physical exam can help document that forced sex occurred and other factors that will be necessary for the case to be prosecuted, if that occurs.

Medical attention is also important because it can provide a victim with a pregnancy test. This can establish whether she was pregnant prior to the rape and thus if she later becomes pregnant as a result of the rape. Medical care can also test for sexually transmitted diseases. These test results may not be available immediately, but are important for the victim's recovery because, as she attempts to put her life back together, she must also deal with whatever physical complications, if any, have resulted from the assault. The decision to seek or not seek medical help also re-establishes a sense of control in the victim. Regaining control of her choices is a major factor in promoting a victim's recovery.

Legal Intervention

A rape victim who presents herself to a hospital for medical care will probably be encouraged to report the crime to the police. Many do not, particularly when the assailant was an acquaintance. Many victims are embarrassed, others are fearful, and still others think they will never be believed and may even themselves be doubtful of the credibility of their own stories. In this respect, validation by notifying law enforcement can make a victim feel empowered. She is no longer helpless but can take action and pursue her attacker and bring him to justice. Often the decision to seek legal recourse, either through the criminal justice system or through a civil action against the assailant, comes as recovery begins.

A victim's initial reaction to a rape is usually one of shock, denial and fear of retaliation from her attacker if she reports the crime. She has to be prepared to endure endless questioning and be willing to describe over and over again the painful details of the attack. If victims are not yet ready to be interrogated and are unprepared to deal with doubts, their recovery may be impeded by being subjected to cross-examination of their character, sexual habits, integrity and personal history. Yet if the crime is not reported immediately, the likelihood of ultimately convicting the offender is diminished. Rape trauma syndrome is therefore important to explain the relationship between delays in reporting and the process of recovery. It is both a sign of recovery occurring and part of the recovery itself to have the ability to choose to accuse one's assailant and endure the inquiry and criminal trial that may follow.

Privacy And Publicity

Few victims of rape are confronted with the concerns of privacy and publicity that met the accusers of William Kennedy Smith and Mike Tyson. Despite the fact that most women are not victimized by such public figures, a woman who reports a crime must be prepared to deal with possible publicity, particularly if she is in a small community, her assailant is well-known locally or the attack was particularly brutal. The victim needs to decide whether the publicity offers a constructive opportunity or whether it is an unwelcome intrusion and she should refuse to participate. Each victim needs to decide for herself, based upon her own needs and circumstances.

A victim also needs to determine who she personally would like to notify about the attack, and then do so. Often this causes her great anxiety, particularly with respect to telling her husband, lover or significant other. As a result, this task is sometimes assumed by law enforcement or medical personnel. The consequences of having them do this are both positive and negative. On the positive side, the victim is spared the initial shock and anger of family and friends, who are then able to acknowledge the crisis and regroup before coming to her rescue. On the negative side, victims must always strive toward re-empowerment, and to do as much as possible for themselves. To the extent that a victim feels too anxious or fearful about the attack to notify her most trusted allies, she may be giving in to her feelings of helplessness and defeat.

Task 4: Rebuilding And Reorganizing

Several days after **Beth** was raped by Jerry, she still couldn't return to her apartment where the attack occurred. She was staying with her friend, Debbie, and each time she thought about going back, she became fearful and anxious and would decide to stay a few more days. Beth also found herself refusing social activities and at times had trouble even getting herself to work. Beth gradually became more and more withdrawn and less willing to talk even with Debbie about the rape. Ultimately Beth felt she was imposing too much on Debbie and had to leave. She found a new apartment and moved with the hope that this would help her regain control of her life.

After a victim goes through the acute phase of rape trauma syndrome and sustains its emotional challenges, she begins to reorganize her life. Since the key to a victim's recovery process is becoming re-empowered, she should not be prevented from making whatever changes or alterations in her lifestyle that she needs in order to regain control.

Reminders Of The Attack

Many victims of rape report feeling dirtied and defiled. They may need to bathe excessively, throw out the clothes they were wearing or the bed sheets if they were attacked in their own home. They may be afraid of dark places, being left alone or going out alone. They may be fearful of certain situations or certain types of people. They may be unwilling to date, engage in social situations or resume sexual relations with a partner.

Recovery during this stage of the trauma includes validating rather than confronting the victim's fears, helping her understand what has happened and allowing her to indulge herself in whatever (reasonable) measures make her feel safer, better about herself and, particularly, more in control.

Adjustments To Lifestyle

Many victims of rape change their residences, their telephone numbers or their daily habits or routines. Depending on where the rape occurred, they may try to avoid the location or other obvious reminders of the event. Particularly at this stage of a victim's recovery, she should be encouraged to make whatever reasonable adjustments to her lifestyle that make her feel more comfortable and in control.

Resuming Activities

As the victim begins to resume her activities, she is also likely to begin to suppress or deny the long-term effects of the sexual assault. This is the second "disorientation" phase of rape trauma syndrome. Even if the victim experiences such common occurrences as flashbacks, she may become less willing to talk about the rape experience or how it has affected her life. Often she seems to be engaged in an almost heroic effort not to be victimized but to regain her dignity and emotional integrity and walk away from the experience.

Intervention on behalf of the victim is difficult during this phase. Denial of the victimization may be strong and an unwillingness to acknowledge long-term effects is not unusual. The victim may simply want to "get on with her life" and resume its normalcy. The acute crisis has ended and the long-term effects are not yet apparent.

During this phase the victim often fails to follow up with medical care and becomes less vehement about pursuing her assailant through criminal justice channels. She may also be less willing to talk about the event, particularly how it is currently affecting her. She may continue to question her own participation and wonder if she was too seductive, too careless or too naive. She may also want to shed the image that she has been defiled or devalued because of the rape. These may, in part, be some of the reasons that she is less willing to discuss the event further. Another reason may be that she has found family and friends to be somewhat ambivalent about her victimization or even outright hostile about her participation or "asking for it." If her support network during the acute phase of the trauma was lacking or unhelpful, the victim is also unlikely to continue to reach out.

Task 5: Integration

Two months after *Elaine* was raped by her ex-husband, she had made substantial progress toward reclaiming her life. She received medical attention and her assailant was going to be prosecuted. She had also "worked through" a lot of the shame and blame feelings and was beginning to come to terms with what had happened. She could not, however, resume much of her sexual relationship with her current husband, Paul, despite his patience as she came to terms with her trauma. Each time he would come near her, she would relive her feelings of anger and helplessness and would blame Paul for being aggressive and needy. This often led to her rejecting him. At times she would recognize that she was projecting her anger at her attacker onto Paul and could respond to him. More often, however, his advances made her feel invaded, angry and insecure.

But that realization didn't seem to help her control her anger and depressed actions.

The most obvious indication that a rape victim is moving into the final phase of rape trauma syndrome is that her outward appearance of "everything is fine" is not consistent with her inner feelings of depression and emotional instability. Feelings of anger or inability to cope may be triggered by finding out that she is pregnant, has contracted a sexually transmitted disease or perhaps has been called upon to participate in a court proceeding against the defendant. Even if there is no identifiable precipitating event, the victim may become aware of this phase of the syndrome when she finds herself plagued by thoughts of the assault without any apparent reason.

The central issues that constitute the focus of the phase called "reorientation" revolve around the victim's feelings about herself and her attacker. If, for example, the victim still feels guilty or ashamed about not having prevented the assault, she needs to talk about what happened, how it happened and what she might have done about it. The value of this type of interchange is not to try to convince her that she was helpless or blameless, but to help her reach her own conclusions about what her participation was and whether she had any power to change the course of events.

Usually the victim will herself conclude that she did not have any power to change the events and therein lies the benefit of her being able to work through those issues. In the event that she concludes that she did do something that was ill-advised or used poor judgment, she needs to come to terms with what that was and not magnify or distort her participation. Even if she concludes that she does have reason to feel guilty or ashamed, there are limits to those feelings and they need to be understood so that they eventually become integrated and the victim can move forward.

Issues surrounding the victim's feelings toward her assailant are more difficult to work through but are the other important part of this phase of the recovery process. During the acute phase of rape trauma syndrome, the victim is usually aware of feelings of anger, hostility and revenge. They are processed and expressed along with feelings of shock and disbelief, but her anger toward her rapist is clear and she will usually verbalize it.

With the onset of the second phase, the initial feelings of anger and despair were suppressed and denied, only to re-emerge now during the integration phase in order to be worked through. What complicates the process, however, is that instead of seeing these feelings of anger against the attacker for what they are, the victim often turns them inward against herself. She is generally depressed and processes most thoughts and feelings in terms of helplessness and hopelessness. Thus the same basic thoughts that led to feelings of anger and blame of the rapist become anger and blame of herself.

This final phase of rape trauma syndrome, particularly if handled competently by an experienced professional, can often be resolved relatively quickly, assuming that the victim's anxiety and/or depression is not of such magnitude as to require extensive therapeutic intervention. The "resolution" of this phase is to understand not only what happened, but how it affected the victim. If she is having sleep disturbances or a change in appetite, she needs to know why it is happening and that it is "normal" or expected. Similarly if her reactions appear to be within a normal range, she also needs to know that something more may be going on. Determining if the victim's reaction is within the expected parameters of rape trauma syndrome is usually made based upon whether her depression seems to be related to the assault *per se*, whether she makes reasonable progress over time and whether there are any psychotic features accompanying the depression.

If there are psychotic features present and progress is limited, this usually indicates that the rape has somehow struck a vulnerable point within the victim or stirred up a previous trauma that the victim is now re-experiencing in an exacerbated form. The development of psychotic features will present a barrier to the victim's being able to cope with the more current source of her distress. If this is the case, the victim needs to be referred for professional care, usually including a psychiatric evaluation.

During the "reorientation" phase, work will also be done to manage the victim's symptoms, usually depression, irrational fears or suspicion and sexual dysfunction. Assisting her in understanding the relationship between the trauma and the symptoms will go a long way in helping her to come to terms with her experience and "integrating" those experiences into her life. She cannot and should not be expected to somehow "forget" about the attack or pretend that it has not had any effect on her life. It does, and it likely always will. Nevertheless, there can be some positive outcomes of even the most painful of experiences, and she needs to find out what these are for her.

For some, learning greater caution can contribute to feeling safer in the future because they incorporate this new information and implement better safety measures. For others, becoming more compassionate of other victims who share their plight and reaching out to them with a common bond is therapeutic. For them, this is a healing experience and they feel that they are accomplishing a useful function. In doing so, they become part of a new network of individuals with a purpose, who come together with a common ground and desire to make a difference. They may form or join support groups of rape survivors or other similar networks.

For still others integration comes through the knowledge gained from their experience that they can then share with others. This may occur through an active involvement in educating people about rape or through the sharing of individual experiences with their close friends. In addition, the need to deal with the effects of being raped may provide a victim with the opportunity and motivation to address other traumas which have occurred earlier in life and have gone unresolved. This type of individual "integration" of the rape trauma may lead to the "integration" of other life traumas.

In all cases the greatest hallmark of a victim's recovery is that she becomes empowered once again to take control of her life and does not feel relegated to a life of victimization. For some this occurs when she decides to pursue legal action and not unduly fear her attacker. For others it occurs when she is able to resume most of her normal activities. And for still others it occurs when she succeeds in reaching out and helping another woman in need. What is important is that a victim use the process of recovery to find out what empowers her, and through that empowerment, the will to achieve recovery.

Task 6: Recovery For Family And Partners

When *Nancy* was raped by a co-worker whom she had brought back to her apartment one evening after working late on a project, her first response was to call her fiance, Jeff. He had always been strong and supportive whenever she found herself in difficulty and she was sure she could count on him to help her through this crisis. When she first spoke to him, his response was cool and deliberate. He agreed to come over and assist her in whatever she needed. However, when he arrived, he seemed distant and unsympathetic, almost as though he had been the one violated. As time went on, it became clear to Nancy that Jeff had doubts about Nancy's participation in the rape and wondered what else she had been doing with this man in her apartment.

Kathy and her husband, Peter, had always had a good sexual relationship prior to Kathy's being raped by a man she had been friendly with years before her marriage. After the rape, Kathy had difficulty responding to Peter's sexual advances and Peter, who had tried to be calm and supportive concerning the assault, was also beginning to lose interest in Kathy. The wife with whom he had always had a good physical relationship now seemed to him to be distant and unattractive. He never really understood exactly how the attack had happened and he wondered how she must have felt about this old friend.

An important part of a rape victim's recovery concerns the resumption of her social and sexual relationships. Many women find themselves uninterested in social situations and even fearful of them, particularly if such an event led to her assault. Many women also find it difficult to sustain their sexual relationships even with a partner or establish a new relationship if they were not involved prior to the rape. Men and women react differently concerning their ability to carry on sexual intimacy after a sexual assault. For women, the difficulty is part of the rape trauma syndrome and, as such, follows the phases of the syndrome. The last stage of reorganization and integration includes recapturing the ability to feel sexually intimate with an appropriate male. The process is difficult, takes time and requires that the woman undergo a substantial part of the healing process and feel that she has regained control of other parts of her life. As the rape becomes "integrated" into her life, she begins to feel able to resume her prior activities, including the potential for sexual intimacy.

The question of how partners of victims of sexual assault respond to the aftermath of such a trauma is more difficult. There is no identifiable "rape trauma syndrome" for them, although they clearly have their own emotional reactions to the assault. Rape is a crime of both violence and sex. It is also an act of both physical assault and injury upon another person and an act of taking, if only temporarily, the use and possession of the victim's body. The rapist wants both to have and to hurt his victim at the same time. And the way that he wants to have her is in a sexual way. This is what makes it difficult for a husband or boyfriend to accept. In this regard partners of acquaintance rape victims may have a more difficult adjustment than those whose partners were victimized by a stranger.

As in the previous examples the partners often wonder what the victim might have done to provoke the attack. They may wonder whether she was somehow seductive, inviting or perhaps deserving of the outcome.

Even when a woman is victimized by a stranger, her partner is likely to have a strong negative reaction to the assault, and it is likely to affect their relationship with one another. Men have difficulty accepting that a woman has been sexual with another man, even when she was clearly the victim of a brutal attack. She has still been "possessed" by another and the rapist has taken from the partner something that was exclusively his, her sexuality. Even when a man believes that the woman was not at fault, he still has difficulty accepting that the incident happened according to her account. Further, if by chance the woman lost her virginity to the rapist, the male will have an even more difficult task in accepting that she is not now permanently "damaged."

What type of intervention is available for men who also feel victimized by a rape? They, too, need to have their feelings about the assault validated. The focus of care and compassion is rightfully on the victim. She and others around her do not typically attend to the partner until well after the incident when he has already experienced significant effects. Often men feel that they are somehow responsible for not preventing the attack, either because they should have been available or because somehow events should have been organized differently. Men need to work through their feelings of helplessness and come to see that their guilt is unfounded. Once again, they need not be told of this. They need to be assisted in reaching this conclusion themselves.

Men also need to have their own feelings of victimization understood. Men are so often reluctant to express themselves at all, particularly when it is their girlfriend or wife who is in crisis. The couple need to know that a sexual assault is a crisis for both of them and that the man's experience of pain and loss is also real. If he questions whether the woman somehow induced or participated in the assault, he needs to verbalize his concerns and allow them to be addressed. This is true even if it is determined that his speculation is unfounded. In short, men and sometimes the entire family system need to have available to them whatever resources are necessary to assist them with their reaction to the crisis.

The successful resolution of the rape experience is contingent upon the victim's ability to shift from seeing herself as a victim to seeing herself as a survivor. The ultimate goal is for the survivor not merely to accept what happened to her, but to come away from the experience with a new view of herself, an enhanced sense of meaning to her life and a feeling of mastery and empowerment.

AFTERWORD

As this book goes to press, two important cases have come to the authors' attention. In Maryland a woman charged her estranged husband with rape and presented to the jury a videotape of the alleged act in which it was clear that she was bound and gagged with heavy tape and that forcible intercourse occurred. The husband's defense was that this was their usual form of sexual activity and that it was consensual, in that when his wife said "no," she usually meant "yes," even though this event occurred on the night of their separation. The court found that there was reasonable doubt about the consent issue and acquitted the defendant. In a subsequent television interview, the only juror who would allow herself to be interviewed stated that the jury voted to acquit because they did not feel that the offense warranted a prison sentence.

In Pennsylvania, a female student was allegedly raped on a college campus and pressed charges against her assailant. At the subsequent trial both the victim and the accused testified that the victim had said "no" to sexual intercourse. Here again the defendant was acquitted. This time the finding of reasonable doubt was on the issue of whether the woman's saying "no" really meant "no."

These two cases have received much media attention and their verdicts appear to strike a cynical and depressing chord for those who are concerned about violence against women.

One is, however, reminded of the ancient Chinese temples which are guarded on either side of their entrances by statues of frightening and unattractive mythical animals. Why would a temple, a holy place, have such representations at its entrance? The reason, we are told, is that the ancient Chinese knew that before one can enter the domain of enlightenment, one must pass through the mire of confusion. The creatures represent confusion, the temple enlightenment.

Thus these cases, which appear to portray an absence of understanding of the suffering of women, may be held as representation of confusion. As our society increasingly is presented with the magnitude and severity of the violence perpetrated against women, there will be much confusion. Some will be generated by ignorance and some by disbelief, denial and perhaps even violence. These exist as the desire to deny that problems still exist and good answers still elude us. To continue to deny will be increasingly more difficult as courageous women come forward and risk telling their stories. They will force society to face itself and initially a great deal of confusion will ensue. These two cases represent the confusion in which our society currently finds itself. Those who have experienced the violence or know of others who suffer may look at the outcomes of these cases with anger, but not with despair, for these cases tell us that society is being confronted. The outcomes tell us that there is much confusion. History tells us that with courage and knowledge, confusion will be alleviated, then creative and effective solutions will be identified and implemented.

APPENDIX

Directory Of Rape Victims' Resources

There are increasing numbers of resources available to the rape victim, but the type and availability may vary from state to state and even among communities within a single state. To identify resources in your own community, a good place to start is by looking up "Rape" in your telephone book. You can also call your local police station to ask for the number and location of the nearest Rape Crisis Center. (You can still maintain your anonymity and privacy in so doing.) Other hotlines, such as Suicide Prevention or Runaway Hotlines, as well as the emergency room of your local hospital, can provide a referral.

There are also a number of national organizations that you can contact in order to identify local resources or later if you would like to become a member and participate in efforts to deal with the problem of rape in a more comprehensive way.

National Resource Groups

National Coalition Against Sexual Assault
Albany County Rape Crisis Center
199 State Street, No. 640
Albany, NY 12207

(Contact NCASA if you are interested in membership, or if you are looking to network or locate other rape crisis centers in Connecticut, Maine, New Hampshire, New Jersey, New York, Pennsylvania or Vermont.)

National Center for Prevention and Control of Rape
National Institute of Mental Health
Room 6C-12, Parklawn Building
5600 Fisher Lane
Rockville, MD 20857
(To request a free directory of rape crisis programs around the country, contact NCPCR.)

National Clearinghouse on Marital Rape
2325 Oak Street
Berkeley, CA 94908

National Organization for Victim Assistance
1757 Park Road, N.W.
Washington, D.C. 20010

National Coalition Against Domestic Violence
1500 Massachusetts Avenue, N.W., Suite 35
Washington, D.C. 20005
(NCADV has a list of shelters all over the country that is constantly updated.)

Women USA 1-800-221-4945
(A toll-free number which has taped information about particular political issues which affect women.)

National Women's Political Caucus
State Chair
188 Church Street
Newton, MA 02158

National Organization for Women
P.O. Box 7813
Washington, D.C. 20044

National Organization for Women
Legal Defense and Education Fund
132 West 43 Street, Suite 200
New York, NY 10036

The National Victim Center
2111 Wilson Boulevard, Suite 300
Arlington, VA 22201
Tel: (703) 276-2880

Center for Women's Policy Studies
2000 P Street, N.W., Suite 508
Washington, D.C. 20036-5997
Tel: (202) 872-1770

National Criminal Justice Reference Service (NCJRS)
Box 6000
Rockville, Maryland 20850
Tel: (301) 251-5500 or
    (800) 851-3420

National Center on Child Abuse and Neglect (NCCAN)
330 C Street, S.W.
Washington, D.C. 20201
Tel: (202) 245-0586

Clearinghouse-NCCAN
P.O. Box 1182
Washington, D.C. 20013
Tel: 1-800-FYI-3366

National Maternal and Child Health Clearinghouse
38th & R Streets, N.W.
Washington, D.C. 20057
Tel: (202) 625-8410

Children's Defense Fund
122 C Street, N.W.
Washington, D.C. 20001
Tel: (202) 628-8787

Chesapeake Institute, Inc.
1141 Georgia Avenue, Suite 310
Wheaton, MD 20902
Tel: (301) 949-5000

The Association of American Colleges' Project on the Status and Education of Women
1818 R Street, N.W.
Washington, D.C. 20009
Tel: (202) 387-3760

National Coalition Against Domestic Violence
P.O. Box 34103
Washington, D.C. 20043-4103
Tel: (202) 638-6388

Clearinghouse on Family Violence Information
P.O. Box 1182
Washington, D.C. 20013
Tel: (703) 821-2086

National Clearinghouse for Defense of Battered Women
125 South 9th Street, Suite 202
Philadelphia, PA 19107
Tel: (215) 351-0010

National Coalition Against Sexual Assault (NCASA)
2848 Ontario Road, N.W.
Washington, D.C. 20009
Tel: (202) 483-7165

National Center on Women and Family Law
Room 402 - 799 Broadway
New York, NY 10003
Tel: (212) 674-8200

National Legal Aid and Defender Association (NLADA)
1625 K Street, N.W.
Washington, D.C. 20006
Tel: (202) 452-0620

Women's Legal Defense Fund
2000 P Street
Washington, D.C. 20036
Tel: (202) 887-0364

American Civil Liberties Union
1400 20th Street, N.W.
Washington, D.C. 20036
Tel: (202) 457-0800

The National Crime Prevention Council
1700 K Street, N.W., 2nd Floor
Washington, D.C. 20006
Tel: (202) 466-6272

King County Rape Relief
Box 300
Renton, WA 98057
Tel: (206) 226-5062

International Society for Traumatic Stress Studies
435 North Michigan Avenue, Suite 1717
Chicago, IL 60611-4067
Tel: (312) 644-0828
Fax: (312) 644-8557

National Clearinghouse for Alcohol and Drug Information (NCADI)
P.O. Box 2345
Rockville, MD 20852

National Aging Resource Center on Elder Abuse
810 First Street, Suite 500
Washington, D.C. 20002
Tel: (202) 682-2470

National Victim Center
307 West 7th Street, Suite 1001
Fort Worth, TX 76102
(817) 877-3355

BIBLIOGRAPHY

Balos, Beverly and Fellows, Mary Louise. "Guilty of the Crime of Trust: Nonstranger Rape," *Minnesota Law Review*, 75 (1991), 599.

Bart, P.B. and Obria, P.H. **Stopping Rape: Successful Survival Strategies.** Elmsford, N.Y.: Pergamon Press, 1985.

Berger, V. "Man's Trial, Woman's Tribulation: Rape Cases in the Courtroom," *Columbia Law Review*, 77 (1977), 1-123.

Bhirdo, Kelly W. "The Liability and Responsibility of Institutions of Higher Education for the On-Campus Victimization of Students," *National Association of College and University Attorneys*, 16 (Summer, 1989), 119.

Brown, Valerie L. "The Campus Security Act and Campus Law Enforcement," *West Education Law Reporter*, 70 (January, 1992), 1055.

Brownmiller, S. **Against Our Will: Men, Women and Rape.** New York, N.Y.: Simon and Schuster, 1975.

Burgess, A.W., ed. **Rape and Sexual Assault II.** New York and London: Garland Publishing, 1988.

Burt, M.R. "Cultural Myths and Supports for Rape," *Journal of Personality and Social Psychology*, 38 (1980), 217-230.

Chappell, Duncan; Geis, Gilbert; and Geis, Robley, eds. **Forcible Rape: The Crime, the Victim, and the Offender.** New York, N.Y.: Columbia University Press, 1977.

Estrich, Susan. **Real Rape.** Cambridge, Mass.: Harvard University Press, 1987.

Evans, Mary C. "The Missouri Supreme Court Confronts the Sixth Amendment in Its Interpretation of the Rape Victim Shield Statute," *Missouri Law Review,* 52 (1987), 925.

Goode, S. "Where a Boyfriend Becomes No Friend," *Insight* (April 20, 1987), 58-59.

Gordon, Margaret T. and Riger, Stephanie. *The Female Fear.* New York, N.Y.: The Free Press, 1989.

Graham, Kenneth W. "State Adaptation of the Federal Rules: The Pros and Cons," *Oklahoma Law Review,* 43 (1990), 293.

Groth, A.N. **Men Who Rape: The Psychology of the Offender.** New York, N.Y.: Plenum Press, 1979.

Kanin, E.J. "Date Rape: Unofficial Criminals and Victims," *Victimology,* 9 (1984), 95-108.

Kilpatrick, D.E.; Resnick, P.A.; and Veronen, L.J. "Effects of a Rape Experience: A Longitudinal Study," *Journal of Social Issues,* 37 (1981), 105-122.

Meyer, T.J. "Date Rape: A Serious Campus Problem That Few Talk About," *Chronicle of Higher Education* (December 5, 1984).

Muehlenhard, C., and Linton, M. "Date Rape and Sexual Aggression In Dating Situations: Incidence and Risk Factors," *Journal of Counseling Psychology,* 34 (1987), 186-196.

Murphy, Sakthi. "Rejecting Unreasonable Sexual Expectations: Limits on Using a Rape Victim's Sexual History to Show the Defendant's Mistaken Belief in Consent," *California Law Review,* 79 (1991), 541.

Myers, M.B.; Templer, D.I.; and Brown, R. "Coping Ability of Women Who Become Victims of Rape," *Journal of Consulting Clinical Psychology*, 52 (1984), 73-78.

Nadelson, C.; Notman, M.; Zackson, H., et al. "A Follow-up Study of Rape Victims," *American Journal of Psychiatry*, 139 (1982), 1266-1270.

O'Leary, Kathryn A. "Evidence - Defendants' Sixth Amendment Right to Confrontation Becomes Discretionary Under Sexual Assault Counselor-Victim Privilege," *Suffolk University Law Review*, XXI (Winter, 1987), 1222.

Parrot, Andrea. **Coping With Date Rape and Acquaintance Rape.** New York, N.Y.: The Rosen Publishing Group, Inc., 1988.

Parrot, Andrea and Bechofer, Laurie, eds. **Acquaintance Rape: The Hidden Crime.** New York, N.Y.: John Wiley and Sons, Inc., 1991.

Rapaport, K. and Burkhardt, B.R. "Personality and Attitudinal Characteristics of Sexually Coercive College Males," *Journal of Abnormal Psychology*, 93 (1984), 216-221.

Rowland, Judith. **The Ultimate Violation — Rape Trauma Syndrome: An Answer for Victims, Justice in the Courtroom.** New York, N.Y.: Doubleday and Company, 1985.

Silverman, Daniel S.; Kalick, Michael S.; Kalick, Edbril; and Kalick, Susan D. "Blitz Rape and Confidence Rape: A Typology Applied To A 1,000 Consecutive Cases," *American Journal of Psychiatry*, 145 (Nov. 1988), 1438-1441.

Smith, Michael Clay. "College Liability Resulting From Campus Crime: Resurrection For In Loco Parentis?," *West Education Law Reporter*, 59 (May, 1990) 1.

Torrey, Morrison. "When Will We Be Believed? Rape Myths and the Idea of A Fair Trial In Rape Prosecutions," *University of California Davis Law Review*, 24 (Summer, 1991), 1013.

U.S. Department of Justice. **Intimate Victims: A Study of Violence Among Friends and Relations.** Washington, D.C.: Government Printing Office, 1980.

Yaroshefsky, Susan. "Balancing Victim's Rights and Vigorous Advocacy for the Defendant," *Annual Survey of American Law* (1989), 135.

New Books . . .
from Health Communications

HEAL YOUR SELF-ESTEEM: Recovery From Addictive Thinking
Bryan Robinson, Ph.D.

Do you have low self-esteem? Do you blame others for your own unhappiness? If so, you may be an addictive thinker. The 10 Principles For Healing, an innovative, positive approach to recovery, are integrated into this book to provide a new attitude with simple techniques for recovery.

ISBN 1-55874-119-4   **$9.95**

HEALING ENERGY: The Power Of Recovery
Ruth Fishel, M.Ed., C.A.C.

Linking the newest medical discoveries in mind/body/spirit connections with the field of recovery, this book illustrates how to balance ourselves mentally, physically and spiritually to overcome our addictive behavior.

ISBN 1-55874-128-3   **$9.95**

CREDIT, CASH AND CO-DEPENDENCY: The Money Connection
Yvonne Kaye, Ph.D.

Co-dependents and Adult Children seem to experience more problems than most as money can be used as an anesthetic or fantasy. Yvonne Kaye writes of the particular problems the co-dependent has with money, sharing her own experiences.

ISBN 1-55874-133-X   **$9.95**

THE LAUNDRY LIST: The ACoA Experience
Tony A. and Dan F.

Potentially The Big Book of ACoA, *The Laundry List* includes stories, history and helpful information for the Adult Child of an alcoholic. Tony A. discusses what it means to be an ACoA and what the self-help group can do for its members.

ISBN 1-55874-105-4   **$9.95**

LEARNING TO SAY NO: Establishing Healthy Boundaries
Carla Wills-Brandon, M.A.

If you grew up in a dysfunctional family, establishing boundaries is a difficult and risky decision. Where do you draw the line? Learn to recognize yourself as an individual who has the power to say no.

ISBN 1-55874-087-2   **$8.95**

3201 S.W. 15th Street,
Deerfield Beach, FL 33442-8190
1-800-441-5569

**Health
Communications, Inc.®**